András Gerő

THE JEWISH CRITERION IN HUNGARY

Translated from the Hungarian by
Alan Campbell

Social Science Monographs, Boulder, Colorado
Center for Hungarian Studies and Publications, Inc.
Wayne, New Jersey

Distributed by Columbia University Press, New York
2007

EAST EUROPEAN MONOGRAPHS
NO. 701

Originally published as *Zsidó szempontok*

47 Cecilia Drive, Wayne, New Jersey
07470–4649
E-mail: pastorp@mail.montclair.edu

Library of Congress Control Number 2006926412
ISBN 978-0-88033-599-7

Printed in the United States of America

CHSP
HUNGARIAN STUDIES SERIES
NO. 12

CONTENTS

PREFACE

This book consists of five essays.[1] All are about Jews. And about non-Jews. It could not be otherwise: with the waning of the medieval world, the rise of the bourgeoisie and the advent of secularization, professionalization, and assimilation, the Jews were released from ghetto life and the exclusive hold of Judaism. Jews changed. Their lives and destiny were determined by new relationships, new affiliations and—frequently—new confrontations.

In the modern age, Jews lost the distinctive common history and sense of identity which had hitherto provided the framework and substance of their existence. Their identities diverged. Some wanted to preserve everything from older times, others wanted to—and did—break away. Then came the moment when the chosen self-identity counted for nothing: a common history was forced upon them once again by the logic of origin and race. But an enforced common history was not able to keep together what was had broken apart. After the Holocaust, the divergent story continued, as it does today—but with a shared sensitivity to everything that derives from the Holocaust.

What prompted my interest in the story of Hungarian Jews in the nineteenth and twentieth centuries, and in previous interpretations of that story, is what I sensed as problems. The problems formed into questions, to which I sought answers.

There are innumerable potential problems and questions.

I wanted to investigate why public debate has been confined to the dichotomy of assimilation and dissimilation. What about integration? If this question was not expressed at the time, is it possible to formulate it in retrospect? Can suitable language and terminology be found for something that probably existed but was not mentioned as such? What

about the symbolic Jew? What does he symbolize, and why? How did Jewish identity shatter? And if it has disintegrated, is there some kind of leftover Jewish essence? Is it possible to establish a Jewish criterion? If so, what is it? If not, then why is it mentioned, and what is understood by it? Is origin the most important aspect? Could a viewpoint that declares itself Jewish actually borders on the anti-Semitic construct?

Miklós Radnóti, one of the outstanding Hungarian poets of the twentieth century, was considered Jewish by the anti-Semitic Hungarian government of the time. He was also considered Jewish by Jews who believed in the power of origin. But Radnóti himself did not consider himself Jewish. For me, this is a problem. Or several problems at once. It is easy to make a mistake. We may wrongly perceive the problems; formulate questions wrongly; or find the wrong answers. And we may make the mistake of badly expressing what we want to say.

Nobody has a prerogative in erring. Everybody can do it. I am no exception. At the same time, I am sure of the existence of the problems, and I am sure of my questions. I am somewhat less confident as regards the answers. I am partly affected by intellectual inhibitions, but more importantly, I do not believe in the "right" answer. I prefer to think that I may become part of a long-standing, and still wide-open, discourse. Because the real answer is the discourse itself. This can also help us, perhaps, in ultimately saying properly what we want to say. Perhaps.

CHAPTER ONE

JEWISH PATHS—HUNGARIAN LIMITS IN THE NINETEENTH CENTURY

LIBERALS, ANTI-SEMITES, AND JEWS AT THE BIRTH OF MODERN HUNGARY

The spring of 1848 promised the advent in Hungary of "liberty, equality and fraternity." The twenty years of gradual progress, known as the Age of Reform, and the relentless struggle for the country's bourgeois transformation, in parallel with changes in Europe, had finally come to fruition. The revolt of 15 March and the will of the parliamentary assembly in Pozsony [Pressburg, Bratislava] gave the impression that nothing could stand in the way of the notion of equality before the law.

But the universality of liberty was challenged in the first days. Anti-Semitic riots broke out in Pozsony on 19 and 20 March, as they had a month earlier, sparked off by the granting of full civic rights to Jews in the city. Anti-Semitic protests were not restricted to Pozsony, and continued in April. Jews found themselves facing the horrors of pogrom-inclined anti-Semitism in Szombathely on 4 April, Székesfehérvár and Pécs on 5 April, and Pest on 19 April. The public meeting in Pest resolved that (1) payment of rents should be waived for a quarter, since there had been no earnings during the month of revolt; (2) the situation of the workers should be improved; (3) Jews should be driven out of the country; (4) Jews should not be admitted into the national guard.

The sweeping demands, and the idea that bound them together, cast some doubt on the unqualified popularity of equality before the law in

Hungary. This was the background to poet Sándor Petőfi's complaint, written in the wake of disturbances following the events of 15 March:

> The harmony which has so far prevailed without exception in the capital is beginning to fall apart. German burghers, I denounce you before the nation and future generations for being the cause of its disintegration! May both pass judgement upon you.
>
> It was they who first declared that they would not recruit Jews to serve alongside them in the national guard, and they who first flung mud on to the virgin pure flag of 15 March!...Or do not the words still hold true, did you not cry out with us: liberty, equality, fraternity?[1]

The anti-Semitism which in Pozsony had degenerated into a pogrom by Easter Monday (23 April) prompted the most prominent liberals to take open action. Mór Jókai, Antal Csengery, József Bajza, and Zsigmond Kemény all spoke out against the anti-Jewish provocations, and Hungary's "poet laureate" Mihály Vörösmarty, wrote in an article published in May under the title *The Jewish Question:*

> There can be no more bitter mockery of the proclamation of equality and fraternity than the hatred and rage which have raised their fists against the Jewish people throughout the world, though perhaps most savagely in our country. After the first few untainted days of freedom, in which the noblest pearls of human emotion bubbled to the surface, the dregs are now showing their face, making counterfeit claims to plunge the shining ideal of civil society into darkness. After freedom had bravely stood up for its inalienable rights, lawlessness could not remain silent, demanding the waiving of rents and the division of land, and many violated the peaceful process of petitioning by setting out, in the name of equality, to batter and plunder the Jews, first of all.[2]

The liberal intelligentsia responded to this anti-Semitism with unanimous and unqualified rejection. On the other hand, liberal politicians and the liberal parliament—to quote Vörösmarty—took action with an "irresolute hand."

Kossuth himself wanted to postpone equality under the law for Jews, calling on them to "be patient a little longer in the interests of the homeland and the freedom of the people."[3] He justified his standpoint by saying that, although what had occurred was distressing, prejudice was a reality against which "the gods themselves contend in vain." Behind this position probably lay the conviction that for the sake of the reconciliation forming up among different interests, a sacrifice had to be made, even if this put a question mark against the whole process.

Naturally, not everyone shared Kossuth's views on the need for an important sacrifice of principle in the interests of practical politics. Samu Bónis reacted to Kossuth in the National Assembly by saying, "it is impossible to share the view of those swayed by unrest; legislation may not be dictated by sordid street demonstrations, but by justice and principle alone. The heroes of disruption must be punished, not honored in contempt of justice."[4]

The liberal and democratic intelligentsia raised their voice in vain; similar views were pressed without result in political circles; the advocates of postponement prevailed. Only on 28 July 1849 did the National Assembly adopt the law on emancipation of the Jews, on the same day as the law on nationality—scarcely two weeks before the already inevitable defeat.

Hungarian Jews reacted to the twofold challenge of 1848—faced with calls for emancipation on one hand and the unprincipled policy of delay on the other—in a twofold manner. The anti-Semitic atmosphere of spring spawned bitterness and disillusion. An office was set up by Ede Horn, Adolf Dux and others encouraging Jews to emigrate to the United States, the land of freedom and equal rights. This reaction soon faded, however, and a significant number of Jews who had been pushed out of the national guard enlisted in the Hungarian army. The emigration office became a recruiting office.

Liberal efforts to secure emancipation and anti-Semitic moves to deny it; impulses towards both assimilation and dissimilation: this was the dilemma at the birth of modern Hungary.

THE LIBERAL PROPOSAL: ASSIMILATION

For Hungarian liberals, the question equality before the law for Jews was not new: the Lower House had already raised it in the 1839–40 diet with a view to granting them parity with other groups outside the nobility. (The bill failed to overcome the resistance in the Upper House, but not without some gains. Act XXIX of 1840, entitled "On Jews," allowed Jews to settle freely except in mining towns, and Ferdinand V's decree of 27 July 1846 abolished the special tax levied on Jews, facetiously known as the "tolerance tax.")

The liberal advocacy of emancipation will not be traced in chronological detail here. More interesting is what inspired them, since this was largely what determined the specifics of assimilation.

Valuable evidence is provided by the speech of Baron József Eötvös to the Upper House during the 1840 parliament, which he also published as an extended essay.[5]

Eötvös's argument, fully expressing the view of Hungarian liberalism at that time, takes as its point of departure the view that,

> the time has come when the legislature should extend its caring hand to this unfortunate section of the populace; it is the message of the time, calling for the embourgoisement of the people, a new affirmation of our progress, shining evidence of the progress this House is proceeding towards liberty. In the firm conviction that a free constitution may only be built on justice applied equally to every class of people and on full respect for all human rights, and in the knowledge that the fate of this people hangs on the sense of justice of this House, I may perhaps make so bold as to declare that the time has come in which the Jews, too, may look to a better future within this realm.

It was a powerful argument, based on the formula of combining values and interests. Freedom and equality before the law were linked up to the notion of rational self-interest. Eötvös believed that the granting of equality before the law to Hungarian Jews would ultimately strengthen the position of the Hungarians, constituting as they did a minority in the country:

> The objection is advanced that [the Jews] have until now shown no inclination to join the Hungarian nation. They do not consider themselves true citizens in a country where they have always been regarded as aliens; they have not become united with a nation which has treated them with contempt; and they have little zeal for a constitution known to them only as a burden. Reflecting upon this, my astonishment at those who raise such an objection is matched only by my pity for those against whom it is directed. Should we wonder that the downtrodden do not find common cause with the nation?...The German provinces of France, which in the course of a century have become French, and England, where so many different peoples have come together as a single great nation, stand as evidence, clearer than any argumentation, that the most diverse peoples can unite into one great whole whenever and wherever the same rights centralise separate parts. In Holland, France, England and the United States, nobody accuses the emancipated Jews of a lack of national identity. No one will be able to accuse them of this in our country either, as soon as their emancipation renders them full and free members of our nation, whereupon, by gaining a homeland, they will be capable of affection for that homeland.

Hungarians would thus be ethnically strengthened by the adoption of liberal values—the nation would increase in numbers and strength. The question remained, of course, as to what the new members of the nation would be like. Would they become Hungarian in character too?

Eötvös did not ignore this question, particularly because the opponents of emancipation cited the alleged negative characteristics of Jews, most of these connected with the commercial activity held in such contempt by the feudal order. Eötvös argued that offensive behavioral traits were linked to oppression, and would disappear along with it. On the question of commerce, he declared, "I dare say that the orientation of Jews towards commerce is rather a consequence of their persecution. Having been forced to take this direction they attained perfection in it. I would venture to assert that on becoming full citizens, Jews will find new routes open to them, so that this purely commercial inclination will

diminish rather than strengthen...." This did not, however, resolve the question of what emancipated Jews should be like, a question which grew more complex in the run-up to the emancipation act of 1849.

The pursuit of Hungarianization through emancipation found itself up against two major demands. The first arose from the specter of mass immigration. This was liable to slow down the process of making Hungarians out of Jews, if not render it impossible, especially if the process itself set off another great wave of immigration. Thus a demand arose for regulation, not to say curtailment of rights.

But there was another demand, which powerfully expressed the essence of Hungarian liberalism at that time: namely that the Jews, in order to be accepted into Hungarian society, should make changes in their religious practices and customs, the Jewish behavioral traits associated with these, and in the rules or standards which set Jews apart from the rest of society, i.e. if they wanted to get out of the ghetto, they should change their Jewishness too.

Acceptance of the Jews was thus—explicitly or implicitly—linked to conditions, which in turn were linked to the main point of acceptance, the strengthening of the Hungarian nation. To put it another way, the close interweaving of liberal values with perceived national interests resulted, by reaction, and from the very beginning, in the setting of decidedly antiliberal constraints.

This peculiar state of affairs acquired clear expression in the formulation of the symbolically important emancipation law adopted on 28 July 1849. The bill introduced by Bertalan Szemere states:

Art. 1: As regards religious differences between citizens of Hungary, no distinction being made, the principle shall be applied that any resident of the Jewish faith who was born or has legally settled within the borders of the Hungarian state shall enjoy all political and civil rights pertaining to the citizens of any other religious faith.

Art. 2: The conditions of settlement shall be defined by the government in a temporary decree.

Art. 3: Marriages between persons of the Jewish and Christian faiths shall be declared valid in respect of their civil consequences. Such marriages shall be contracted before the

civil authorities and their procedure shall temporarily be defined in a decree.

Art. 4: The minister of internal office shall permanently be charged with the following:

a) Citizens of the Jewish faith shall call an assembly made up of their clergy and representatives to consider reforms to their ecclesiastical apparatus in concordance with needs of the present age.

b) This act renders obligatory that persons of the Jewish faith shall be directed by means of suitable rules to the practice of manual trades and agriculture.[6]

The implications of the act were twofold. Since civil equality before the law could only be complete if it includes religious acceptance, Jewish emancipation necessarily implied full-scale liberalism; the act thus went beyond civil and political equality to institute civil marriage, and so indirectly religious acceptance. On the other hand, articles two and four, although given as accessory considerations rather than preconditions, pointed in a different direction. The requirement for regulation of "legal settlement" in fact affected immigration policy, and could take effect only if the Hungarian government was sovereign and able to decide whom to admit into the country and whom to exclude from it. Such a sovereign decision was not possible if the Hungarian state was part of a larger empire. This consideration is worth noting because of the significance it took on in 1867.

Of more pressing relevance, however, was religious reform, or rather the resolution to restructure Jewish society. The latter implied that the liberal state, accepting civil and political equality, must in some way interfere in the free choices of its emancipated citizens. (Several twentieth century measures did just this, and not just to Jews; the higher education restrictions, the administrative constraints imposed through chambers of commerce, and the labor camp system are notable examples.) If the state was to steer a particular group of its supposedly free citizens along predetermined courses, it would no longer be liberal, having violated the principle of equality before the law. This section of the act was therefore illiberal—and indeed unenforceable if the state wished to maintain respect for the principle of equality before the law.

The requirement of religious reform was not unequivocally illiberal, however, because the law called for its promotion rather than for its imposition. If the representatives of the Jews wanted religious reform, then so be it. The law merely expressed the executive power's expectation that such reform should take place.

If we wish to interpret the aims both of those wishing to expand or to harmonize civil rights and of those who wanted to restrict them, it is not enough to view the Hungarian liberals simply as politicians struggling within the confines of preexisting prejudices.[7] The demands imposed on Jews—whether preconditions or auxiliary factors—are related to a prime issue in Hungarian liberalism, one that concerned not so much Jewish affairs as the status of the Hungarian nation.

The main purpose of emancipating the Jews was to strengthen the Hungarian nation. This was a particularly pressing consideration in a country where the majority of the population belonged to other ethnic groups. The fundamental, consciously-identified objective of Hungarian liberalism was to create, via equality before the law, a nation in the civil sense of the word. The creation of a nation was inextricable from liberalism, but this pursuit of modernity, by eroding the feudal concept of nationhood, inevitably highlighted and fuelled the issue of ethnic affiliation, since it might set off similar processes among the non-Hungarian national groups which constituted the numerical majority. The building of a modern nation also added further points of conflict to Habsburg-Hungarian relations, since the prospect of Germanization, already threatening feudal privileges, presented a danger to the whole extended nationhood concept, and conversely, the demand for a nation-state threw into doubt the unity of the Habsburg empire.

The development of the cultural nation concept (language reform, the Academy of Science, grammar, national literature, etc.) was gradually accompanied by a political nation concept based on liberal codes of law which, although offering no collective rights to the country's various national groups, promised—and where possible, conferred—broad individual rights. It was thought that individual rights would provide sufficient cohesion to counterbalance collective national movements.

In this context, Hungarian liberals could not base their national consciousness on a culturally integrative view of society. On the con-

trary: they wanted to impose a Hungarian mold on other groups so as to homogenize them with the nation. The liberal nation concept formulated in terms of homogenization rather than integration logically excluded the notion of cultural diversity, and its proponents did all they could to give Hungarian culture, or what they regarded to be so, an identifiable form. Since the Jews did not have a national identity of their own, they constituted an ideal subject for assimilation. (This had already been recognised in Vienna, where the Germanization policy forced Jews to assume German family names.) However, although they may have lacked a national consciousness, the Jews had a religion whose all-embracing nature posed a challenge to the notion of assimilation. Not confined to principles and guidelines, Judaism prescribed rules governing all aspects of life from eating habits to married life. It was an entire culture affecting everyday customs as well as religious life. This was somewhat incompatible with the concept of a historically-evolved Hungarian nation having a homogeneous, rather than an integrative, culture. And since this different culture was, or appeared to be, inextricable from the Jews' position in the division of labor, the latter was also called into question and became a target for change.

This serves to explain why liberalism demanded that Jews take on Hungarian identity in the cultural sense, as well as the political and linguistic, and why this demand was set into legislation. Furthermore, it is symbolic that the 1849 act linking emancipation to cultural assimilation was passed on the same day as the one granting only partial integration to ethnic minorities in the Hungarian state.[8] It is understandable that, after 1849, it was Kossuth who emerged from the ranks of the Hungarian liberals to espouse unconditional equality before the law, and who in 1851 committed to paper a draft for a new constitution envisaging an integrated society based upon cultural autonomy at the state executive level.[9] By then, of course, he was in exile.

Although liberal Hungarian politics even following the Compromise of 1867 did not change its concept of homogeneity, Jewish assimilation was not the subject of legislation. The law passed in December 1867 consisted of only two clauses. The first stated that "the country's Israelite residents shall henceforth be entitled to exercise all the civil and political rights enjoyed by Christian residents." The second stipu-

lated that "all laws, customs or decrees to the contrary are hereby abolished."[10] No mention was made of immigration, religious reform or state direction of occupations. Their absence was not due to a liberal change of mind: a variety of causes played a part. The terms of the Compromise prevented the Hungarian parliament from ruling on immigration or inhibiting the movement of capital or labor within the empire.[11] As for state-enforced alterations to the occupational structure, the legislators of 1868 probably realized the impossibility of enacting them without taking entirely illiberal measures. There was an initiative on religious reform put forward by the minister of education, but this could not be formulated as a legislative principle.

It was by omission that the desire for full cultural assimilation was most clearly expressed. The 1867 law made no reference, even indirectly, to make Judaism a received religion (religio recepta), and the legislature postponed decision on civil marriages until the 1890s. The practical effect of this was that the main vehicle of Jewish culture was excluded from the emancipation process. This—taken together with the ministerial proposal for religious reform—again implied the linking of emancipation to cultural homogenization, i.e. assimilation.

Although the wording had changed, the proposal from Hungarian liberalism was therefore the same in 1867 as it had been in 1849: become Hungarian and you will be part of the nation. You must, however, give up your own cultural standards and habits. If you do this, we will do more than admit you, we will actually accept you.

A significant number of Jews took up this offer.[12] They made a political commitment to the Hungarian nation, took to speaking Hungarian, and progressively molded themselves to Hungarianness in terms of customs, lifestyle and principles. The Jewish burgher wanted to be a Hungarian gentleman, and regaling himself in the trappings of Hungarianness was not an uncomfortable imposition but longed-for goal. The choice was made easier by the fact that the secular process of embourgeoisement, even without pressure towards assimilation, came into increasing conflict with the regulations of religious traditionalism. The liberal offer was consciously aimed at encouraging Jews not merely to modernize their cultural identity along secular lines, but to renounce it. Jews at various stages along this route responded by vigorously declaring their Hungarianness in terms that went beyond lan-

guage or loyalty to the homeland. They affirmed that Hungarian culture was their own.

Hungarian liberalism's fear of the Germanizing power of Habsburg rule and of the predominance of other nationalities, and the concept of homogeneous culture and national identity it gave rise to, put such a pressure on the Jews that a large segment of them appeared willing to abandon gradually their own cultural identity in order to become Hungarian citizens. They thought that if they remained only symbolically Jewish, they could and would be Hungarian citizens of equal status.

THE ANTI-SEMITIC PROPOSAL: DISSIMILATION

At the birth of modern Hungary in the spring of 1848, the movement towards political emancipation and assimilation was accompanied by the appearance of anti-Semitism, an ideology seeking to exclude Jews from full citizenship.

In its 1848 form, however, it had no intellectual strength; it was not yet a modern ideology that could form a worldview. This had to wait for international influences, mainly German and Austrian, and indeed for the commencement and increasing momentum of the assimilation process.

In Hungary, anti-Semitism as a fully-fledged political ideology started to make itself felt in the mid–1870s.[13] A separate political party formed up around it and gained representation in the Hungarian parliament. The issue from which it drew the most attention—even from abroad—was the Tiszaeszlár ritual murder indictment of 1882. Several Jews were charged with ritual murder of a young Hungarian girl, and the initial verdict of guilty was ultimately overturned by the Royal Supreme Court on 10 May 1884. However, I would contend that the medieval anti-Judaism manifested in this infamous affair was not the key factor. Anti-Semitism drew its new power from the novelty of functioning as a political ideology, and as it confronted the process of emancipation, it formed up around the pursuit of dissimilation. It is thus worthwhile taking a look at the views it expressed—views which were repudiated at the same time.[14]

The modern incarnation of anti-Semitism was troubled principally by the successes of assimilation, coupled with an aversion to the social and material restructuring caused by industrialization and embourgeoisement.

Its point of departure was that Jews were not capable of assimilation because of ingrained racial characteristics. This implies at the outset that Hungarians formed an ethnic-racial category which excluded absorption of any group that did not "originally" belong to it. The Jews—invading the body of the nation through emancipation—lived like parasites (in the anti-Semitic jargon, practicing "stock market liberalism") and debilitated the nation (the reasoning here was based on the Austrian Professor August Rohling's Talmud forgeries). Spurred on by radical German anti-Semitism of Wilhelm Marr and Karl E. Dühring, they claimed that the racial qualities of the Jews—"greed," "duplicity" and "lack of patriotism"—were irreconcilably opposed to the essential characteristics of the Hungarian nation: "chivalry," "openness," and "an honest personality." The Jews grew rich through the pursuit of unproductive forms of business, such as trade and finance: it was rare indeed to find a Jewish brakeman or train conductor. A favorite simile used to portray the relationship between the Jews and the Hungarians was that of "marauding wasps who rob the industrious bees of their honey."

Liberalism presented an opportunity for the "wasps"—Jews—to prevail and so, following this logic, liberal politics favored only the Jews. But not even that was enough for the Jews, whose destructive nature gave rise to other schemes. Jews were inducing morally pure Hungarians to "rum drinking, cigar smoking, and other kinds of extravagance." By means of the economic power they had acquired, they were corruptly seizing control of the judiciary, public administration, parliament and government.

As if control of the entire state apparatus was not enough, Jews were trying to seduce the whole of society to take up the same kind of infamy. It was liberal freedom of the press that they exploited for this end. There were basically two kinds of newspapers: Jewish or "Jew-friendly." "The Jewish press exercises tyranny over public opinion, the crushing of which is the duty and right of every honest patriot," they wrote.

The Jews were effective in their foreignness, repugnance, and destructiveness because they had a power structure, partly open and

partly secret, whose hierarchical cohesion amplified the power of their efforts. (The operation of this organization was conceived along the lines of the autonomous Jewish communities in Russia, the Kahal.)

The assimilation process—a phenomenon theoretically impossible under the anti-Semites' basic premise—was explained as being nothing more than a sham. The total alienness of the Jews therefore had to be exposed. A good example was the Jews' use of the Hungarian language. It was true that more and more Jews were speaking Hungarian, but the result was "degradation" of the language—urban people were speaking differently from rural people, and this was all due to the Jews.

The conclusion was the same as the initial premise: Jews had not and, indeed, could not become Hungarian. They were no more than foreign bodies built into the nation, parasites by nature. Their assimilation was merely a mask behind which they were establishing their own positions of power in the Hungarian state. And their own religious and cultural rules prevented them from seeking true acceptance, they were determined to stay separate. They were drawn by their coreligionists around the world, and were thus irredeemably cosmopolitan and entirely incapable of Hungarian patriotism.

What could be does to stop this contagion? Modern political anti-Semitism offered several recipes which could be applied in parallel. Their favorite proposals were those aimed at restricting or stripping away civil rights. Above all they demanded the revocation of emancipation. Immigration also had to be stopped, and Jews were to be encouraged to emigrate. Laws were also needed to prevent "racial intermingling." These might be supplemented by a numerus clausus (legislating the number of Jews admitted to university, for example) and a numerus nullus (admitting none at all). Anti-Jewish laws on money changing and usury were also considered useful, and the withdrawal of moving rights also seemed like a good idea. Christian social campaigns might supplement legislative initiatives, such as the "Don't buy from the Jews" drive, and it was of course essential to set up a dedicated press.

The logical conclusion of this race-based, antiassimilation Hungarian anti-Semitism was Jewish emigration and the expunging of Jewish influence. Hungarian anti-Semites addressed the question of what the subsequent fate of these outcast Jews should be. Győző Istóczy, at the

24 June 1878 session of the Hungarian parliament, stated that the medieval solution to the Jewish question—mass executions—was not really practicable, and called upon the government to do all it could towards the creation of a Jewish state in Palestine, to which Hungarian Jews could be deported. The Hungarian anti-Semites were ahead of almost everybody else in the world with this idea, flatly contradicting, of course, their assertion that the Jews' racial characteristics rendered them incapable of statehood.

The anti-Semites thus worked on the premise of ethnically-racially determined cultural homogeneity, in contrast with the liberals, who also based their views on homogeneity, but of a kind that could be learned and adopted. They both rejected integration; their differences stemmed from their respective aims of assimilation and dissimilation. Both basic positions, with all their internal contradictions, rested on exceptionally powerful frameworks of ideology, consciousness and language. One might even say they constituted a polar field in Hungarian consciousness and self-expression. Someone alluding to the separateness of Jewish culture might either face the accuzation of anti-Semitism or be a target of the anti-Semites. But a Jew who disavowed—and cut himself off from—any kind of Jewish cultural affinity, although fulfilling the requirements of Hungarian liberals, was forced to deny any cultural heritage in religion or some kind of secularized form, sometimes at the price of lying to himself and to others.

The effect of this absorption-rejection polarity, based on different kinds of homogenization and homogeneity, on the consciousness of the time is illustrated by the following passage about Tivadar (Theodor) Herzl, who trod the path of assimilation first with the Hungarians and then the Germans (or "Austrians," as referred to here). The author was Stefan Zweig, a Jewish writer looking back during the Nazi era. Through his own experiences and times, he evokes the world of the 1890s, the period following the Dreyfus affair, a phenomenon which affected Jews throughout the Habsburg empire:

> Indeed in his upright and manly pride Theodor Herzl had already suffered under the Jewish lot when he was a student; moreover by his prophetic instinct he had foreseen the entire tragedy of his race at a time when it had not appeared to be an inevitable fate. With the

feeling of being born to leadership, which his imposing presence no less than his grandiose thinking and his worldly knowledge seemed to confirm, he had then formulated the fantastic plan to end the Jewish problem once and for all: Jewry was to unite itself with Christianity by means of a mass baptism. Always thinking dramatically, he had pictured to himself how he would lead the thousands and thousands of Jews of Austria, in an exemplary symbolic act, in long procession to the Cathedral of St. Stephen, there to absolve the persecuted, homeless people of the curse of separation and hatred for all time. Soon he realized the unfeasibility of this plan, and years of his own work diverted him from the original problem of his life, the solution of which he had recognized as his true task. But now at the moment of Dreyfus's degradation the thought of the eternal exile of his people entered his breast like the thrust of a dagger.If separation was inevitable, he said to himself, then let it be a complete one. If humiliation is to be our constant fate, then let us face it with pride. If we suffer because of our homelessness, then let us build our own homeland! And so he published his pamphlet, "The Jewish State," in which he proclaimed that all attempts at assimilation and all hope for total tolerance were impossible for the Jewish people. They had to create a new homeland of their own in their old home, Palestine.

I was still in the *Gymnasium* when this short pamphlet, penetrating as a steel shaft, appeared: but I can still remember the general astonishment and annoyance of the bourgeois Jewish circles of Vienna. What has happened, they said angrily, to this otherwise intelligent, witty and cultivated writer? What foolishness is this that he has thought up and writes about? Why should we go to Palestine? Our language is German and Hebrew and not Hebrew, and beautiful Austria is our homeland. Are we not well off under the good Emperor Franz Josef? Do we not make a decent living, and is our position not secured? Are we not equal subjects, inhabitants and loyal citizens of our beloved Vienna? Do we not live in a progressive era in which in a few decades all sectarian prejudices will be abolished? Why does he, who speaks as a Jew and who wishes to help Judaism, place arguments in the hands of our worst enemies and attempt to separate us, when every day brings us more

closely and intimately into the German world? The rabbits thundered passionately from the pulpits, the head of the *Neue Freie Presse* forbade the very mention of the world Zionism in his "progressive" newspaper. Karl Kraus, the Thersites of Viennese literature, the master of invective, wrote a pamphlet called "The King of Zion," and when Theodore Herzl entered a theater, people whispered sneeringly: "His Majesty has Arrived!"

At first Herzl could rightly feel himself misunderstood—Vienna, where he thought himself most secure because he had been beloved there for so many years, not only deserted him but even laughed at him. But then the answer roared suddenly back with such force and such ecstasy that he was almost frightened to see how mighty a movement, already growing beyond his control, he had brought into being with his few dozen pages. true, it did not come from the well-situated, comfortable bourgeois Jews of the West but from the gigantic masses of the East, from the Galician, the Polish, the Russian proletariat of the Ghetto. Without realizing it, Herzl with his pamphlet had brought to flame the glowing coal of Judaism, long smoldering in the ashes, the thousand-year-old messianic dream, confirmed in the Holy Books, of the return to the Promised land. This is the hope and the religious certainty which have made life worth living for the persecuted and enslaved millions. Whenever anyone—prophet or deceiver—throughout the two thousand years of exile plucked this string, the entire soul of the people was brought into vibration, but never as forcefully as upon this occasion, never with such a roaring and rushing echo. By means of a few dozen pages a single person had united a dispersed and confused mass.

The first moment, while the idea was still a dream of vague outline, was decidedly the happiest in Herzl's short life. As soon as he began to fix his aims in actual space, and to unite the forces, he was made to realize how divided his people had become among various race and destinies—the religious on the one hand, the free thinkers on the other, here the socialist, there the capitalistic Jews—all competing eagerly with one another in all languages, and all unwilling to submit to a unified authority. [15]

THE UNSPEAKABLE DISTINCTIVENESS: INTEGRATION

There can be no disputing that the overwhelming majority of Hungarian Jews during the nineteenth century moved towards assimilation, and this can be attributed to the Hungarian liberals' desire to make the Jews feel at home on top of granting them equal rights. The liberals, motivated by the potential threat of Germanization from Habsburg power and the only gradually diminishing preponderance of national minorities (Jewish assimilation accounting for a large part of the improvement), vigorously demanded Hungarianization of the Jews. In addition to linguistic Hungarianization and loyalty to the Hungarian state and people, Jews were called on to assume full cultural identification. Set against this, the anti-Semites rejected such cultural merger, maintaining its impossibility and necessary artificiality, and thus attacked the very notion of emancipation.

Put most simply, this led to the emergence of two narratives of identity and self-expression frameworks. One declared that Jews were equal with others because they were Hungarian. The other took the position that the Jews should have their rights restricted or even removed precisely because they were not Hungarian and could never become so. This is how it was, how it always had been and how it always would be.

The ideological field generated between these two poles spread through the entire scope of popular thinking. One result was a constant attempt by some Hungarian Jews to prove their complete and perfect assimilation, their unassailable Hungarianness. (This continues to the present day.) It was not a surprising reaction. To have asserted any aspect of Jewish culture would have led to confrontation with the homogenizing efforts of Hungarian liberals and provided grist to the anti-Semitic mill.

In his way—on the conscious level—it was more or less impossible for Jews to attach themselves to Hungary in a way which was integrative, i.e. both retaining and modernizing their own cultural identity. Consciousness of this cultural identity might have revealed itself in the more secular aspects of religion—for instance, by celebrating religious festivals in a form acceptable to Hungarians—but also in secularized standards separate from religion, or to be more precise, in the open pop-

ularization of these norms. Or in other words, the possibility of being Hungarian differently. It cannot be said that dissimilarities did not exist, since the assimilation process itself was envisaged in stages, with identification being achieved by gradual erosion of differences. Neither can it be said that the preservation of otherness is the only way. This is a preconception which would obscure understanding of history. All we can say is that integration cannot become a conscious ambition if the person who might somehow seek it finds no willing partner. The only options remaining are either the ideological overemphasis of assimilation, or the pursuit of dissimilation, made into a consistent scheme by a search for historical precursors. (Anti-Semitism does not derive its strength from the validity of its claims but in its determination to stifle self-expression, and so penetrate the popular consciousness.)

It became difficult for religious or even secularized cultural identity to assume an autonomous articulation and thus establish itself as an idea which could inspire the requisite cultural—and, where required, political—organization. It became difficult to be Hungarian in another way, difficult for diverging dimensions of consciousness to develop in juxtaposition and equal value.

Another consequence was the effect this polarization of consciousness had on Jewish and non-Jewish writers dealing with the history and destiny of the Hungarian Jews. Instead of objectively appraising and interpreting events, they became prisoners of the language and concepts of an ideological tangle they were caught up in themselves.[16]

This is particularly striking in the problem of integration. No one denied, either directly or indirectly, that the Jews represented a living culture and that certain religious or secular standards played an important role in their lives. But because scholarly approaches fell into only two categories—homogeneous acceptance and homogeneous rejection—integration could not be consciously formulated as the subject of historical research. (That this is more than just a methodological dilemma is proved by historians' universal practice of mentioning the Jewish origins of protagonists in historical and cultural developments. If the subtle, multi-level "integrative" factor did not exist, then why mention this aspect so consistently?)

My conclusion is that in search of objectivity and fullness of explanation, we must rethink the history of the Hungarian Jews—like so much

else—and give expression to something that was permitted to exist by our history, but was prevented from attaining a conscious, expressible form.

Of course, this is more than a matter of subjective resolve, intellectual thoroughness, or accumulating facts. There is a far more vital preliminary condition. Just as the Hungarian national consciousness—guided by liberal thinking—became capable of regeneration, the same ability today, and—in some ways building on the legacy of Kossuth—the Hungarian nation, both as concept and reality, must be interpreted in terms of cultural integration as well as homogeneity alone. It was a change in Hungarian national consciousness that afforded Hungarian Jews opportunities for self-definition in the past, and a similar scenario is called for today. Only a transformation of such magnitude could put an end to an ideological dichotomy which has already exhausted its resources.

CHAPTER TWO

THE SYMBOLIC JEW, OR WHY DON'T JEWS GO TO HEAVEN?

In the beginning—according to an old story—a long, long time ago, all kinds of people had their places in heaven. They went peacefully about their everyday affairs, until somebody cried out, there's a clearance sale in hell! At that, the Jews jumped from their places and abandoned the celestial empire, rushing headlong for hell. St. Peter shut the door behind them. That is why there are no Jews in heaven, and they can never get back.

This traditional anecdote appears in the *Hungarian Folk Tale Catalog.*[1] Hungarian researchers have recorded five basic versions of the tale. The first was found in Bihar County in 1878, and the last in Tolna County in 1972. Like most folk motifs, this little story is not confined to Hungary, and can be found in international catalogues.

The story, in the course of its century-long career passed from Bihar, through Szatmár County and Upper Hungary even to Transdanubia. To have kept it going so long, and propagated it so far, the storytellers and their audiences must have found it accurate and witty, and so worth passing on. It thus merits some deeper study.

The story seems to say that a person of utilitarian thinking is excluded from the higher benefits. Utilitarianism is base, heaven is good and beautiful. The kind of person who is drawn to profit draws ridicule; his greed disqualifies him from the finest things that may be granted to man—if only after death. In this anecdote, the Jew is a symbol, or a symbolic figure. The content concerns utilitarianism, and not Jews in the first instance. This naturally prompts the question as to why this set of values is assigned to the Jews.

Taking a more general view of the representatives of utilitarianism, we come to a hybrid Latin-Greek expression, "homo oeconomicus."

This literally means "one who manages his wealth," but actually goes further than this, referring to motivation and method. It is normally used to mean the kind of person who acts in his economic interests, led by the profit motive, and who attempts to gain the highest profit with the smallest investment. In this sense, "homo oeconomicus" represents a definite value system and form of behavior and implies a complete way of life and outlook. Such a utilitarian person can only evolve when and where there is the possibility of pursuing such behavior. It must be close to the truth to link the phenomenon historically to capitalism and the rise of the middle class, and we cannot go far wrong if we regard its spread in a particular society, and the changes in how it is popularly regarded, as a measure of the extent of the middle class. This little story therefore says much more than its authors, tellers and audience might think: it is really putting the question of why "homo oeconomicus" is ridiculous and "unnatural" and finally: why it is personified in the Jew. Or to put it in a slightly different way, and more generally: why is the basic mentality-characteristic of the middle class so strange and alien?

I cannot promise a full and exhaustive answer in this little piece, since there is a staggering quantity of literature dealing with problem of utilitarianism alone—from Marx to Max Weber, Adam Smith to John Stuart Mill. All I will attempt is a Hungarian historical sketch, with the insertion of a few generalities on which, hopefully, there is a consensus.

A good starting point for an examination of the career of "homo oeconomicus" in Hungary is the time when conscious rise of the middle classes began, the Age of Reform. Count István Széchenyi's famous book *Hitel* [Credit], published in 1830, is of particular interest here. A glance at its list of contents shows that "homo oeconomicus" appears as a thoroughly considered demand, with chapter headings such as "The Hungarian Landowner is Poorer than He Should Be Given His Estates"; "Hungarians Are Less Well Off than Their Circumstances Permit"; "The Hungarian Farmer Cannot Make His Fields Flourish to the Greatest Extent"; "Hungary Has No Trade"; and "What Is To Be Done and How."[2]

These headings convey that values and approaches demanding the utilitarian mentality were assuming a new importance, a hitherto alien idea in Hungary, where the feudal world, from the peasant to the aristocracy, placed importance on completely different values. "Robot" or villeinage was measured not in value, but in time. The obligation of the landowning serf was fifty-two days draught robot or fourteen days labor robot, without any word of intensity or efficiency.[3] The feudal world made its measurements in rank, title, legal status and—in equal legal position—wealth, but did not calculate the ratio of energy invested to the returns gained. What was cherished above all was permanence, and not the kind of dynamism engendered by "homo oeconomicus."

When Széchenyi raised his voice in favor of economy, he was speaking for a new kind of man, and a new kind of behavior. This is not just an interpretation: he himself—as in the processes that had taken their course in western Europe—was much concerned with moral philosophy. He was constantly looking for answers to the question of how the Hungarian noble could become a noble Hungarian, just as eighteenth century British moral philosophy (Thomas Reid, Jeremy Bentham, and Adam Smith) had constantly pondered the possible ethics of human behavior based on utilitarianism.[4] Just as in Britain (and France) in the eighteenth century, the ethics of "homo oeconomicus" emerged as a clearly-defined issue. It was not just a matter of drawing up a new set of norms to replace the feudal worldview. It was at least as important to create within utilitarianism a kind of normative, moral brake on excesses in everyday acts. This was to stop "homo oeconomicus" from degrading into an extreme individualist, or more precisely, an egoist: a value dictator with no regard for the rights of others, casting aside or even destroying others in pursuit of his own interests.

To create a harmonious moral face for the new type of bourgeois man was never going to be easy. But there can be no doubt that middle-class values started to emerge and be adopted in Hungary, and however problematic the practical application of a code of ethics, nobody doubted that "homo oeconomicus" was the only way forward. Indeed, even Hungarian "moral philosophy" did not, in my view, seek to reproach, but rather to assist, the formation of this view.[5]

So what was the trouble? If Széchenyi, Kölcsey and Eötvös were so fervent in adapting the new kind of man to Hungarian conditions, in

fact saw him as the only way to promote the bourgeois development so longed for throughout the land, why did it all seem so alien?

All the efforts of the reforming opposition were not enough to make the Hungarian nobility shape itself into men of new outlook and mentality. Having crystallized over the centuries, their inner norms and behavioral stereotypes were difficult to shift, but that was not the main reason why they remained relatively unresponsive to the appeals from so many quarters. Perhaps the most important factor was that the most active and well-informed of the reform opposition elite were largely constrained to politics. They had much less influence in the social sphere, and even less in the economic. This was because the political arena was the main bridgehead for the advance of the middle class in Hungary. That was where the changes were needed to allow the bourgeoisie, in the socio-economic sense, to flex their muscles. As Kossuth said, it was a political question in Hungary as to whether somebody wore a hat of domestically—or Brünn-made felt, since the empire's customs system, so adverse to Hungary, made the supporting of domestic industry a statement of attitude to political power.[6] For example, the reformers considered industrialization—in line with the "homo oeconomicus" outlook—to be very important for Hungary, but in order to promote it, they were constrained to advocate behavior contradictory to utilitarianism, namely, "do not buy cheaper and better from abroad, but goods of more expensive and lesser quality made in Hungary."[7] And all this had to be said in a context of "pipe-smoking intolerance"[8] among nobles who were traditionally uninterested in such issues.

So although they were the political representatives of bourgeois demands, they often expressed economic demands at odds with the liberal middle-class mentality. Such demands, no matter what their political justification, proposed social behavior which did not encourage the nobility to adopt the outlook and values of "homo oeconomicus," since the statement that the choice of what to buy and where was a matter of patriotism rather than profit was a perfect reinforcement of their indolence and insensitivity in this area.

Personal example, of course, carried great weight. However deep the split between his behavior in the political and the socioeconomic spheres, the career of a major public personality could be galvanizing. The conscious promoters of "homo oeconomicus," however, could not

hold up shining examples of success. The *Védegylet* [Society for the Promotion of Hungarian Products], as might have been expected, made political headway, but was an economic flop. Neither did the *Iparegyesület* [Industrial Association] bear out the hopes invested in it. The *Gyáralapítók Társasága* [Factory Founders' Society] was a stillborn experiment and the failure of the *Kereskedelmi Társaság* [Trade Society]—when the secretary ran off with the society's cash—even dented Kossuth's modest assets. (The absconding secretary even fleeced Bertalan Szemere, an emigré wine merchant, this time in England.)

Széchenyi was perhaps the only one who could produce successes that confirmed to the public the values of utilitarianism, but there are several reasons why his was an example that could not be followed. First of all, his great successes were assessed in the national rather than individual terms, since the Chain Bridge connecting Buda and Pest, and the railway were national, i.e. collective, rather than personal victories. Secondly, Széchenyi himself was well known to be caught up in his own dilemmas and thus presented a picture of a completely failed personality. And thirdly, Széchenyi's social position was obviously unattainable to ordinary people, who regarded him with some justification as having exceptional, aristocratic privileges.

The "homo oeconomicus" paradigm was therefore not taken up even by the increasing number of the upper classes who were committing themselves to bourgeois values, at least not on a large scale.[9] It became no easier for the nobility to change their orientation following the suppression of the 1848 revolution, since economic modernization was accompanied by neoabsolutism in politics. Some elements of neoabsolutism, rational enough in themselves, found themselves in a politically deniable context.[10]

On the other hand, the Age of Reform, the failed revolution, and the national public rejection of neoabsolutism drove on the cause of the bourgeoisie with even greater force, even though the political conditions were far from favorable. The conduct which had been urged in the 30s and 40s thus increasingly spread through socioeconomic affairs at a time when neither the political authorities nor the nobility were able to accept it. "Homo oeconomicus" was making a striking entrance, but as "homo novus." The "new man" not only left behind feudalist thinking, he came from a different group and value set than

the existing social elite. Germans, a rising number of Jews, and a decreasing number of Greeks made up the bulk of the repositories of utilitarianism in Hungary.[11] The more settled post-Compromise state and local government system provided the former nobility with an alternative in the form of senior positions in state and county government and public service.

In the bourgeois development of Hungarian society during the Monarchy, two prevailing and partly intertwined "cultural anthropological" fields emerged. This is a somewhat rough aggregation, blurring subtle transitions, but useful for analysis, just as it used to be used for stigmatization.

The mentality in public affairs, and to a certain extent in social intercourse, had become gentlemanly but still essentially feudal. Looked at from our "homo oeconomicus" viewpoint, this conduct existed as the denial of utilitarianism, and even drew its ethos from denial. A Hungarian gentleman was known for "paying like an officer."[12] In that section of society, it was the done thing to spend more than one earned. In individual life, it was a forgivable sin to undertake an irrational risk, whether that be a duel or a whole estate staked on a bet. It was a mentality devoid of bourgeois utilitarianism, built on opposing values and conduct, and was patronizing or hostile to any departure.

These norms had, of course, to be financed by somebody. This noble task fell largely to a section of society which, in terms of economic behavior and of course in private life, lived and acted in accordance with the norms of bourgeois "homo oeconomicus." In public affairs, it largely assimilated to the gentlemanly world, but was different in reality. Its members worked all day, even if they were rich, whether their name was Leó Lánczy or Manfréd Weiss. They did not spend more than they earned and did not take on any more risk than needed. They found their pleasures in calm family life rather than nights on the town. The group did include some sons of "old" families. (Baron Frigyes Podmaniczky, after his family's financial collapse, took on work and was forced to think economically, a dandy only in dress, not in values.)[13]

The two "anthropological faces" of Hungarian bourgeois development may have scowled at each other in secret, but they smiled in public. Jewish businessmen elevated to the nobility and donning ceremonial attire on the one hand and bearers of great historical names indo-

lently officiating board members on the other.[14] Marriage strategies, lifestyle concessions (purchase of estates) and a host of other way-of-life variations indicate the existence of cultural symbiosis among careers built on widely divergent motivations.

The positive feature of this symbiosis was that anticapitalism and bourgeois entrepreneurship could coexist, sometimes in the mind of the same person. The dual personality—ennobled and bourgeois—appeared in many places, but particularly in the outlook and lifestyle of the gentry and the aristocracy. They nurtured the illusion of countryside Hungary, but preferred to live in the city. They despised money that was beneath them, but often hoped that someone would buy them, i.e. that they could sell themselves or their services for money. They needed capitalism, but looked down on and sometimes hated its representatives.

The cultural anthropological medium which emerged and maintained its basic features right up to the end of the World War II, perhaps even up to the present, thus had at least a double structure.[15] Despite borrowing from each other, society was divided into two distinct cultural aspects in terms of personal values and mentality. Put more precisely, it was not a simple division so much as an amalgam that drew its strength from bourgeois development but left the process in a semifinished state, since in the world of public affairs, politics and personal conduct, high social prestige was afforded to those who did not behave as bourgeois, while the bourgeois financers of the structure could only truly be themselves in the areas of financial activity and private life.

This mutually repellent "golden age" symbiosis was easy to undermine and attack. The attacks could equally be championing the cause of bourgeois development or trying to restrain or even suffocate it.

The reaction finally came in the form of the Catholic People's Party, the ideological precursor of the interwar Christian current. From a conservative base, it attempted to stifle even the modest bourgeois development that had taken place. It attacked Budapest as the sinful city (as if there was an alternative to urbanization), held Jewish capital to be parasitic (as if that word did not perfectly fit those who, for socio-political reasons, through a "force beyond the economy" supported themselves on the capitalist mechanism—"anti-homo oeconomicus" par excellence) and advanced the anti-middle-class conception of the-organic "lord-and-peasant unity of Hungarian life."

After the break-up of the Monarchy, both civil democracy and Communism were defeated in the political arena, leaving only the Christian current in the field, expressing its antibourgeois outlook as anti-Semitism,[16] and weakened the coexistence of middle-class and aristocratic social conduct.

Although somewhat late in coming, given the severity of the problem, a movement did emerge in interwar Hungary reflecting the oppressive lack of bourgeois development. Some saw the greatest barrier to the improvement of the peasantry—largely under the influence of the Christian-national current—in the Hungarian bourgeoisie, and were often ambivalent about joining such a movement. Most, however, saw the greatest hindrance to bourgeois development as the combination of great estates and bourgeois property, therefore seeking some kind of populist third road.[17] However, this logically led to a flirtation with both the political current wanting to weaken the existing bourgeoisie and pervaded by anti-Semitism, and various left-wing forces opposed, in various ways, to capitalism itself. (The careers of the prominent writers Gyula Illyés and László Németh display this ambivalence.)

This populist movement was of course greatly motivated by the will to create cultural and mental norms set against gentry, urban and bourgeois values, and establish the positive image of—and represent—multi-suppressed peasant society in public affairs. It identified "Magyar" with "peasant," naturally opening the way for hostility to both Jews and the middle classes, as well as to the traditional political elite. Thus urban culture was declared alien; folk music, beyond its undoubted value, was claimed to be of exclusive significance; and the hymns of praise to work-centred peasant life inevitably implied conflict with "homo oeconomicus." It is therefore not surprising that the capitalist entrepreneur was viewed as a suspicious, wicked figure concerned only with how he could make a profit—and with as little work as possible. This naturally opened up roads towards the left, without offering an actual alternative.

The populists therefore intended to draw up a third face of Hungarian society, set against the gentry and bourgeois faces, and thereby to define the concept of "Hungarian" in terms of their own cultural values. The essence was of course a struggle with the problem of middle-class aspirations of the peasantry, but the prevailing historic and societal

milieu forced this to proceed via multifarious ideological and political meanderings. Many of the ideas may have been cul-de-sacs, many of the leading figures performed drastic political turnarounds, but the movement certainly sprang from what was undoubtedly one of the key threads of Hungarian social progress, and the issue was to a considerable extent kept alive by the internal difficulties of Hungarian bourgeois development. Just as 1848 brought the decisive move in freeing the serfs, a similar attempt was made for land redistribution in 1918. The only difference was that the attempt succeeded in 1848, but withered away (or was killed off) in 1918, even though inestimable energy could have been freed up for Hungarian societal and middle-class development, giving rise to a "populism" of completely different substance.

The aftermath of World War II, despite the enormous destruction, left great opportunities for internal development. Land was at last redistributed, and the old sociopolitical clique was broken up. It is true that a considerable body of the Hungarian middle class had been broken, but there was a good chance that the middle-class development of the peasantry on a mass scale could, if not immediately, galvanize Hungarian society with an unprecedented bourgeois energy and raise "homo oeconomicus" into the accepted norm.

Politics, however, took things in exactly the opposite direction. Aiming to completely eliminate the bourgeoisie, the new regime, for which utilitarianism and its representatives were actually criminal, radically cut short the middle-class potential of the peasantry, because it could only generate capital for its grandiose plans by casting the whole of society into impoverishment and a new kind of serfdom. (It also, logically, followed the pattern of the aristocracy in creating its own nobility and establishing social privileges.) Thus took shape a world of compulsory quotas (corresponding to the tithes of the old order) and "nomenklatura" (corresponding to the high aristocracy, prefects, etc.).

The post-1956 neoabsolutism, with its desire, just like its nineteenth century predecessor, to lift serfdom once again and to respond to middle-class demands, kept up restrictions on political freedom but gave room for "homo oeconomicus" activity. One of its motives was to generate a financial basis for itself. It also attempted to fetter middle-class energies by quiet disdain and administrative restrictions even as late as the 1970s and 80s, when it was making louder and louder dec-

larations of the need for utilitarianism, and ultimately gave way to fatal extravagance without ever actually adopting the bourgeois mentality.

The "gentrified" state apparatus had been left with no alternative but to allow bourgeois development so as to create the resources for its rehabilitation. But a large section of society had descended into a condition (owing to the same policy of restricting "homo oeconomicus") where people were hardly able to assemble any capitalist energy. They were glad to be surviving. Others cast themselves into the new opportunities with spectacular ambition, but not with the least idea of rehabilitating the extravagant state. Why should they weigh down their energies to prop up a system that had been working against them for so long?

Those left out of the new capitalism could easily be turned against utilitarianism, and those who were in it could easily be marked out—through a bit of political propaganda and ideological dressing—as enemies of the people. And then there were the rest, who were completely bewildered. Afraid, confused, sometimes just apathetic.

It seems natural that the ideological reminiscences which were the products of the contradictions and internal tensions of Hungarian bourgeois development—including "homo oeconomicus"—should be revived in such a situation. It is not difficult to detect the partial or full continuity of bourgeois radicalism, the Christian current, socialist values in a new guise, and other orientations. The same is true with the ideologically-assorted populist camp, which combines ideological precedents with a reading of the current situation to identify the enemy and mark out the (first? second? third?) way forward.

Understandable and natural, but not necessarily acceptable. Not just unacceptable because of personal sympathies and aversions. The approach can be governed by much more substantial aspects. For example, a more or less industrialized society cannot be dominated by an archaic, naïve culture. "Homo oeconomicus" can be shunted about and whittled down under this principle or that, but only at a high price. The story of bourgeois development in Hungary has proved by the very tortuousness of its own route that there is no alternative to "homo oeconomicus." There is only the choice between a series of fudges and failures and a full-blown process opening up opportunities for real success.

I see no great problem for the Jew, or rather "homo oeconomicus," who does not get into heaven. What good is utilitarianism in commu-

nist heaven? Few get through the pearly gates in any case, and of course, you have to die first.

It is down here, on earth, where there is a need for wealth.

And if we want to return the symbolic Jew to a symbolically-interpreted historic arena, then by a syllogism Count István Széchenyi could be called the greatest Hungarian Jew.

Chapter Three

THE FRAGMENTATION OF JEWISH IDENTITY

Our concepts often present themselves as ready interpretations. Their casual use saves us much effort by making something appear "self-evident" that would otherwise demand an explanation. The word "Jew" is used as a more or less self-evident identity category, even though the content it conveys has been just as much transformed by secularization, modernization, assimilation and acculturation as any other identity category. Whatever meaning we ascribe to it, the word "Jew" has denoted a minority throughout the diaspora, and as with every minority, what is decisive is the content of the category expressing the majority, and how that content changes.

The question of what is what, and how we define things, is a matter of decoding, or more precisely the means of decoding. For this, of course, we also need the words and concepts by which we attempt to say anything at all.

The means of decoding is history itself. History can be interpreted as the story of society, the course of politics, and as many other things. Such as awareness, identity, self-identity, and classifications of ourselves made or expressed by others. This is true for Jews, Hungarians, and Communists. Seemingly straightforward identities could be ambiguous, and sometimes mutually entangled, or even deliberately confused. Interpretation is more and more difficult, if for no other reason than we also have to interpret the interpreter. The history of our identities is in a certain sense equivalent to us ourselves. And to further complicate the issue, majority and minority (whatever they may mean) contextualize each other, and have to be interpreted relative to each other.

In examining the relationship of the Hungarian national identity to a people originally lacking an autonomous national identity—the Jews—we must not ignore how the subject of our discussion is defined.

JEW

In the world before secularization and the modern idea of the nation—up to the nineteenth century in Hungary—a Jew was somebody of the Jewish faith. The Jewish religious enlightenment in German-speaking Europe reinterpreted much of religion and religious rules, and thus created major differences among believers of the same religion.[1] Followers of the diverging movements may have criticized, indeed vilified, each other, but this did nothing to change the fact that Jewishness meant Judaism, even if there were wider and wider differences as to what was regarded as Judaism. Jews argued and wrangled with each other, but everybody else regarded them as Jews on the grounds of their religion. In consequence, prejudices against Jews was known as anti-Judaism, since it was expressed in the name of Christianity, against Jews as followers of Judaism.

The internal cracks, however, caused the Judaism-based concept of Jewishness in Hungary to fall apart within a couple of decades. By the last third of the nineteenth century, religious identity and self-identity had broken into three distinct groups. [Namely: the Neolog (Reform), Orthodox and "status quo ante" movements.] Depending on the movement they adhered to, Jews went to different synagogues, dressed differently, and led different lives. As Judaism's cracks deepened, Jews in Hungary became divided. Their uniform image in the eyes of non-Jews could, of course, have remained intact, but other changes were taking their effect on the concept of the Jew.

The change was driven by the mutually reinforcing and interrelated processes of secularization and the modern concept of the nation. The Christian universalism of the feudal world was steadily eroded by the new, particular, and at the same time secular concept of the community, the nation. Being a worldly community, the nation did not dissolve the religious differences between people, but reduced them to insignificance in comparison with the former worldview. Insignificance in

effect meant secularization. It was a very bumpy journey, concluding with the ecclesiastic policy laws passed in the early 1890s, when state and church were separated and the state treated the Jewish religion as a "received denomination," i.e. accepted it.

In the eyes of the state, at least, religion became a personal matter, or more precisely it was left to individuals, or free associations of individuals, to form their own worldview. This normative resolution of the matter was accompanied by a much more contradictory process in society, since strong religious constraints retained their hold on marriages and social relations, but the legislation contributed to the breakdown of the old determinacies.

Jews, whose identity was based on religion, had no national consciousness. This left them free to choose, or rather forced them to make a choice, as regards their national affiliations. But national affiliation, as nations took form and the Christian universalism of the feudal world gradually faded, became an identity of increasing importance.

In the 1780s, it was government policy to Germanize the Jews, forcing them to take German surnames. However, since the Germanizing authorities were thinking in terms of imperial rather than national identity, the question still remained open. For Jews without national consciousness, the real challenge was Hungarian identity.[2] The Hungarian national movement involved more than just linguistic cohesion, it held the promise of equal ranking membership of the political community. For the Jews, the promise of equal political rank was of double significance, because they were the only social group without a national identity.

During the Age of Reform, and in 1848, the Jews experienced frequently-varying combinations of existing social prejudices, the tradition of anti-Judaism and the intention of equality before the law. They also experienced how the days of March 1848, with their promises of equality, were followed by riots involving anti-Judaist rhetoric and tending towards modern anti-Semitism. And, of course, they experienced the—somewhat belated—acceptance on equal rank by the modern Hungarian national consciousness when an act of parliament was passed on the issue in 1849.[3]

Beset with pitfalls and setbacks as it was, the process nonetheless gained further reinforcement immediately after the Compromise in 1867,

when equality before the law and emancipation for Jews was specifically enshrined in law.

The possibility and challenge of national identity became an increasingly broader reality under the liberal political disposition in the years that followed. The rising current of assimilation—a term embracing a highly complex set of phenomena—swelled to become the mainstream of Jewish affairs. To understand the religious fragmentation in societal terms, it is useful to examine the appeal of assimilation to the Jews. The power of Neologism grew from national—and thus secular—identification. Jews widely thought of themselves as having become Hungarians, or more precisely Hungarians of the Mosaic faith. The power and depth of assimilation may seem less convincing in retrospect, but the fact remains that more and more Jews in Hungary saw themselves as Hungarians, and were increasingly looked on first of all as Hungarians, and only secondarily as Jews. Just like others for whom national identity was primary, with other considerations—such as being Catholic or Protestant—coming only in second place. It was this momentum of change that created the political conditions for the separation of church and state.

And so the Jews, who had identified themselves by their religion, acquired for themselves a national identity. Still regarded as Jews on the basis of their religion, they nonetheless became Hungarians. They were statistically classified as such, and were regarded as such by members of other nations.[4]

At the turn of the ninteenth and twentieth centuries, however, the picture changed again.[5] It was a two-way change, stemming both from intra-Jewish affairs and from a discourse that reflected various processes and led to a new framework of attitudes.

Many Jews, as traditional Judaism gradually waned and identification with worldly affairs spread, began to regard religious Jewishness as a burden that could be shed. It was a burden in the first place because, even after reforms, it prescribed many regulations obstructing everyday secular life. It was simply uncomfortable. But abandoning religious constraints also made it easier to escape from prejudices against Jews. And on the spiritual side, the personal need for the Jewish religion diminished because it was replaced in many respects by membership in a community.

Individual responses varied: taking Hungarian names became common, and not a few people, after rising in society, actually converted to Christianity in the hope of speeding and securing their rise, and making themselves more firmly Hungarian. And then there came the opportunity to identify with something universal and very secular, going well beyond national particularism: socialism. Its promise and its rituals made it the universal religion of international and worldly redemption, sweeping aside every religious, national and other inherited cultural dimension.

The result was the hitherto unthinkable phenomenon of the Jew who was no longer a Jew. None of this ran to a final consummation, of course, and it was the divergences along the way that lent the traditional view of the process, the fragmentation and disintegration of the Jewish identity its characteristic features. It was a double incompleteness. Firstly, no single approach proved to have sufficient merits to completely eliminate, liquidate or prevent the progress of the other approaches. By the early twentieth century, there were living in the same country the traditionally-recognizable figures of religious orthodoxy, the muscular communities of reformed Jews, ambitious converted "Jews" who made it right up to ministerial rank, socialist ideologist, and more-Hungarian-than-the-Hungarian writers, poets, and patriotic poetasters.[6] Then there was incompleteness of the individual kind. It was possible to take up diverging processes simultaneously, or to vary the tempo, and a single person or family often declined to follow any single route to its conclusion. Socialist-minded young intellectuals pursued their studies with the financial support of families who maintained and cultivated Jewish traditions; the relatives of converted Jews remained Jewish, and intellectuals with Hungarian self-identity actually looked to German culture. There was wide scope for variation, innumerable "inconsistencies." All signs that the concept of "the" Jew had been shattered.

The fragmentation of Jewry was also driven by the challenge of national and secular identities, but these challenges only took effect because of the confirmations they promised in different situations. Departing from traditional Jewish ways was "rewarded" by social and intellectual success. Success took the form of honored position and acceptance within Hungarian society, reputation, high office, or the grant of respect from the newly-entered community. Despite the many

attendant contradictions, fragmentation itself opened the way to everything that had been absent from the traditional life of centuries lived in subordinacy and secondary status within society.

This confirmation in turn brought other consequences, however. In the feudal world, Christendom represented the subordination of the Jewry in the power system in the form of anti-Judaism. Anti-Judaism fitted perfectly as the ideology for deprivation or curtailment of rights, since if Jewishness meant identity with the religion, then the religious argument was enough to "cover" the Jews.

So what was to happen as the traditional concept of Jewishness was disintegrating and Jews were appearing as an unprecedented social success story? The weapon of anti-Judaism could only be deployed against those stuck in traditionalism and thus not even competitors in the capitalizing bourgeois world. For ideas to enforce subordination, constraint and elimination of Jews, a new kind of argument had to be sought—across Europe as well as just in Hungary. The new language of the anti-Jewish discourse was anti-Semitism.[7] It often mixed in elements of anti-Judaism (like the "blood libel") but the real targets were Jews in the mainstream of developing bourgeois society.

Anti-Semitism, however, had to contend with the great paradox that the Jewish community, in traditional terms, had disintegrated. To be effective, it had to imbue that fragmentation with an underlying unity. A narrative had to be substituted for the reality. This narrative appeared in several places, since similar processes were in progress elsewhere in Europe, but featured with particular prominence in the world of the Austro-Hungarian Monarchy. The interesting story here does not concern the form of words, but what was actually said, i.e. the propositions behind them. Not stylistic differences, or certain statements, but the concept of Jewishness.

In this respect, modern anti-Semitism partially followed anti-Judaism and partly went beyond it, presenting Jewishness—which was in fact going through a complete break-up—as a singular societal and mental whole. In its view, the Jew was total. The total Jew was a Jew in every area of life. He ate, spoke and thought as a Jew. A Jew was a Jew even when he was not a Jew. What made him dangerous was appearing to be something when he was in fact something else. Stigmatization was a mechanism not reserved for Jews. Prejudiced thinking led to a simi-

lar way of attributing utter evil by the way of speaking about witches or sexual minorities. But the Jew was not just an absolute entity in the way implied or alleged for other groups by similar ways of speaking. The Jew appeared as a secret, hidden organization and his object was to control everything via a conspiracy pervading the nation and the whole world. In this conception, the "Jewish conspiracy" was immeasurably dangerous because the Jew was absolute while so often being invisible. The anti-Semitic conception varied in nuance, sometimes being strongly explicit, elsewhere somewhat cloaked, but was constant in the essentials. The approach naturally demanded an explanation of the total Jew, and did not hold back from drawing the conclusions. The explanation shifted increasingly in the racial direction, and the conclusions towards demands for restriction and exclusion of people and phenomena interpreted as Jewish.

Just as the traditional Jewish identity was splitting apart, the total Jew idea came into existence that viewed the breakup (the "reality") as nothing more than an attempt to conceal, to mask the absolute.

The consequences of this special duality were manifold, the narrative setting off a widespread reaction. The break-up of traditional Jewry had set off the competitive appearance of Jews in areas where they had not hitherto been present. This, coupled with their attainment of equality before the law in the secularizing world, gave modern anti-Semitism its strength.

One major consequence was the appearance of Jewish ethnic awareness.[8] Those for whom the anti-Semitic narrative and its societal force were proof that assimilation was doomed to failure, and that a return to traditional Jewishness was impossible, started to think in terms of an national alternative to the Jewish concept and Jewish identity. Zionism—whose founder, Theodor Herzl, was brought up in the culture of Budapest and Vienna—conceived Jewish identity as a national identity and attempted bring Jews following divergent routes together through self-identification with the nation. It attempted to bring followers of both Judaism and socialism into the nation, especially since Herzl conceived the society of the future country of the Jewish nation, Israel, as a kind of socialist utopia. At all events, the end of the nineteenth century found Zionism taking its place as another subdivision of Jewry.

Zionism found few supporters, certainly among Hungarian Jews,[9] mainly because another kind of reaction seemed more practical against the attacks and strengths of anti-Semitism. Even Herzl hesitated, one of his visions being that the Jews should convert to Christianity, as if symbolically completing the process of assimilation. However, he accurately perceived that changing religion could not give a relevant response to the increasingly racial basis of anti-Semitism.

The more promising reaction at the time was to continue the logic of social assimilation, which was going on in any case. It was the articulation of the idea that assimilation would better weld together the citizens of the homeland at the societal level, and assumption of the national—Hungarian—identity would do the same politically and psychologically. Hungarian Jewish leaders unceasingly proclaimed identity with being Hungarian, and not infrequently gave voice to Hungarian nationalism.[10] The advantage of this constant assertion assimilative identity was that it obstructed the advance of modern anti-Semitism in contrast with Austria and Vienna which, lacking a national Austrian identity, followed the great German consciousness. But it came at a price—a price that was most sorely paid in the twentieth century.

Overemphasis on the assimilated identity inhibited the development of a truly integrative identity. It also concealed some cracks and incongruities which were arising in the assimilation process at the time—certain aspects of lifestyle and values suggesting that Jews could be Hungarian in ways other than those with whom they were trying to assimilate. A Jew turned baron could take on the full Magyar panoply just as a traditional Hungarian baron did, but there nonetheless remained differences at certain points. A Jewish law student could attend the same university as his Christian fellow-Hungarian, but his legal career would be predictably different for the sole reason that he was a Jew and the other was not. The list of examples goes on, and they are in many cases quantifiable. Even so, in the world of identity policy, actual differences were concealed by assimilative consciousness, and the anti-Semitic reading interpreted them as signs of the enemy. There was no space for Hungarian Jews to express themselves—to either themselves or others—in terms other than just assimilation and anti-Semitism or, in their own view, in terms of assimila-

tion and dissimilation (Zionism). The option of coexistence, i.e. of integration, therefore did not open up.

Its absence concealed the actual differences and embelished, almost exalted, assimilative identity. (For instance, it made it possible to hold up as an example a Jew who achieved professorial status, but covered up the discrimination he encountered, and the ultimate outcome. Or taken from another aspect, the joys and virtues of assimilation were proclaimed, but traditional choices were preferred in marriage strategy.)[11] This absence, or more accurately the failure to articulate and to find a real identity, left the Hungarian Jews almost completely defenseless when state policy ultimately disregarded their assimilative identification.

Hungarian Jews entered the twentieth century with their traditional identity in decay and the concept of the "Jew" having changed both for themselves and the society around them. The change had not swept away what was there before, but created new variants on old themes. Religious consciousness ranged from Orthodox to Neolog, national consciousness from Hungarian nationalism to Jewish nationalism, and lifestyle from the traditional to the fully secular. And some Jews had gone beyond a shift in identity: taking full advantage of the secular world's opportunities, they had abandoned all of these variations and become Christians, atheists, or socialists. Different identities were obviously the result of different similarities, but this is a matter for social history rather than identity history.

The external world encouraged and tolerated this, and often granted confirmation of it. Encouragement, toleration and confirmation ensured the authenticity of a wide diversity and choice of the identities, however aesthetically jarring some or all of them may have been. But while Jewishness was disintegrating, a reaction was developing against Jews that identified as its enemy the total Jew. Aspirations to integration crumbled, and the question from then on was: if Jewish identity has fragmented, but the imaginary creature of the total Jew is being identified as the enemy, what will happen next?

This question could only be answered by the majority, which we will refer to collectively as Hungarians.

HUNGARIAN

Hungarian national consciousness, and Hungarian nationalism, followed without many deviations the same standard structural course of birth and formation as did other nations. What is important here, however, is the kind of national consciousness into which Jews assimilated, and how the internal content of that national consciousness changed in the twentieth century. Let us examine a few important connections.

The defining force in the birth of the Hungarian national consciousness was the inability of a feudal, aristocratic society to satisfy bourgeois needs via the accustomed means of Christian universalism. Bourgeois energies could only be nourished by creation of a new community, one in which as many people as possible had an interest in operating and maintaining it. Privileges had to be spread wider, and in a way that the new form of social organization maximized its own potential.

National identity here meant that the privileged community was replaced by a linguistic, i.e. a cultural community. This process started in the final third of the eighteenth century and continued up to the reform era. It unfolded as the result of much conscious effort, from recognition of the Hungarian language's importance to its adoption as the sole national language (1844). Language reform, Hungarian Academy of Science, grammar, education—an enormous quantity and breadth of effort.

The creation of a nation as a linguistic-cultural community is a phase, a structural element, in the formation of every nation. The process is always accompanied by a sense of internal insecurity, since such a movement opens up a broad area of confrontation. The Hungarian case is no different, but the particular senses of uncertainty—anxieties—which dominate are determined by historical circumstances.

One of the tensions in Hungary was that a nation considered to be extremely backward had to be "raised up" to fit into the course of European civilization. It must be remembered that the first third or half of the nineteenth century was the period of industrialization and creation of the modern conditions, compared with which Hungary's condition was pitiful. The spectacular, fast-moving development "over there" was

seen against "mud and dust down here." There was good reason to fear that if the stagnancy persisted, then the Hungarians would belong to Europe's "Asian" or "Balkan" half. Another worry was that the feudal political structure, which certainly did not help the country's socio-economic development—would not even be capable of protecting it against Habsburg absolutist ambitions. Then there was the fear—as proved by the cholera rebellion in Upper Hungary (Slovakia) in 1831—that peasant discontent might become uncontrollable, and bloody social conflicts might break out. All of these fears firstly pointed to the need to create a new political community, a nation. It was the creation of the nation itself, however, that gave rise to these and other fears. The paramount fear, one already appearing in the process, was that the Hungarian nation, small in numbers and low in strength, could be buried under the pressure of the much larger German and Slav masses. Hungary without a modern nation could perish in backwardness and the nation could perish in the overpowering embrace of other nations.

There was only one solution offering real prospects, and the cultural-based national consciousness found the appropriate response almost immediately, constantly maintaining the fear motif.

This response asserted the insufficiency of thinking in terms of a cultural community alone. There was a need to form political community consciousness at the same time. The content of a political community could be none other than civil liberty. Civil liberty was the only course that could ensure the leading societal role of the existing elite while offering the peasantry—which made up the mass of the country's inhabitants—some real prospects, and something they could identify with. A necessary concomitant of equality before the law and civil property rights was the liberation of the serfs. The national awareness that formed up during the Age of Reform and came to political fruition in 1848–49 thus stretched out along two axes: cultural and political. The concept of being Hungarian was harnessed to the concept of liberty, thus granting the opportunity for affiliation to those who could not meet the cultural criteria. Many who took up arms for the Hungarian cause in 1848–49 could hardly speak the language. In 1849, many people executed by those who suppressed the 1848–49 Revolution and War of Independence, and thus raised to the "national pantheon" as martyrs to the Hungarian cause, would not, in cultural terms, have satisfied the criteria of Hungarian national identity.

The political concept of the nation—"a single political nation"—remained alongside the cultural concept even after 1867, since the same liberty applied to everyone regardless of national affiliation in the cultural sense. There was no national distinction in terms of rights, and the universal value of freedom took expression in the Hungarian political nation.[12] The underlying content of this line of thinking is captured by an expression used by, among others, Lajos Kossuth: "reconciliation of interests." This reconciliation was conceived in three dimensions: power, nationality-ethnicity, and society. The concept of reconciliation of power implied that a constitutional state with a national consciousness steeped in freedom could also stabilize the Habsburg empire. (This conception worked for a while in 1848, before being overwhelmed by confrontation. The Compromise of 1867, however, proved its viability, and the coexistence of Hungarian national awareness, a constitutional Hungary and the empire really did have a stabilizing effect.) The national-ethnic reconciliation was based on the premise that everybody was due the same political rights regardless of ethnic affinity, and this would be sufficient to ensure the peaceful coexistence of differing ethnic aspirations.

It was thought that the "single" political nation based on the indivisibility of liberty could counterbalance national-ethnical antipathies tending to generate division and conflict. This proved false, at least partly. A series of events in 1848–49 and then later, after 1867, showed that the values of shared freedom did not encourage much self-restraint among national aspirations. In 1848-49, some of the ethnic groups came into armed conflict with the Hungarians, a situation which may be termed civil war. The conflict was not so intense with every ethnic group, so that the value of shared freedom had some effect, but it was basically confrontation and tension that predominated.[13] And neither the memory nor the potential continuation of the conflict born then was to disappear thereafter. The liberal Hungarian national awareness underestimated the power of the national aspiration of the kind that it had itself created.

One lesson of 1848–49 was that reconciliation at the levels of power and national-ethnic affiliation is highly problematic. The consequence of this in the formation of Hungarian national awareness was to mark out a potential enemy figure. Imperial power, and its ally in

putting down the Revolution and War of Independence, Russian power, were inevitably fixed as enemies. In the Hungarian political elite, Russophobia had already started to form during the Age of Reform, and was confirmed and strengthened by Russian intervention. The Habsburg-Hungarian conflict carved deep emotional marks and became an integral part of modern Hungarian national awareness, although one of varying potency. Of course, fear of the Russians and antipathetic behavior towards the Habsburgs partly counterbalanced each other. The Russian peril was not seen as potential invasion and subjugation by the tsar, but as the danger of support for Pan-Slavism which might rend the Hungarians asunder. However, the spread of Pan-Slavism and the increase of Russian influence were not in the Habsburgs' interest either, and so the dynasty also meant some protection for the Hungarians against one of their perceived enemies.

This was the point where in Hungarian national awareness the other perceived potential enemy—some of the ethnic groups—was in competition with the other perceived enemy—the Habsburgs. And since the ethnic movements elicited more anxiety and their national aspirations seemed more threatening, a compromise with a dynasty that largely accepted Hungarian demands was preferred over one with the ethnic groups. (The conception formulated by Kossuth in exile, through a different vision of the hierarchy of perceived enemies, was of compromise with the ethnic groups against the dynasty; it remained completely isolated within Hungary.) This of course does not mean that all traces of attitude towards the dynasty as a kind of enemy ceased—the independence opposition of the Compromise era always included this element—but there was always a strong perception of how far this could go, because they also realized that as time went on it would not be the Habsburgs but the national movements which could dislodge the Hungarian political hegemony in the multinational state.

The third, societal, element of the original "reconciliation of interests" concept must also be mentioned. Its realization was strongly related to the power and ethnic dimensions, and it had a strength that could partly counterbalance the difficulties of the other two. Reconciliation of societal interests served a double goal: firstly to deal with potential social conflicts, and secondly to open the way for the Hungarian people to join the national community of liberty.

A definite success was the minimization of potential social conflicts. In 1848–49, Hungarians did not fight Hungarians. In fact the Revolution and War of Independence drew much of its strength—and thus required the massed armies of two great powers to quell it—from the ability of the peasantry to identify with a process which for them had the power of liberation. From their point of view, however, it was just as important that the nation-creating potential of liberty could also be attractive to societal groups without strong ethnic-national awareness. The process was not without setbacks and diversions, such as the anti-Jewish actions in spring 1848 incited by German burghers fearful of their privileges. Nonetheless, the broadening of rights implied by liberty resonated with a widespread desire to break out of subordinate social positions. This resonance was aided by a meeting of interests, since the state of civil liberty granted Jews the equality before the law they had always been denied, and the Hungarian nation thus gained in numbers and strength. For this Hungarian national awareness, the Jew became an ally rather than an enemy, and this was a mutual perception. Of course, such a rational alliance could not immediately override the centuries-long embedding of anti-Judaist prejudices. It is also true that political-conscious openness did not imply social openness. But even so, something had started, which in retrospect is simply referred to as assimilation.

The Hungarian sense of endangerment and the vision of the enemy had several consequences. National identity started to "coagulate," so that regionality had a diminishing role. It continued to provide variety, but was no longer a dividing factor in Hungarian identity. Popular divisions within Christianity, which had hitherto been the hotbed of so many bitter conflicts, faded into the background, although sometimes remained strong in private affairs. Hungarian patriotism proved capable of loosening Catholic-Protestant antipathies. A by-product of this for the Jews was that this loosening effect of patriotism sapped some of the power from the belligerent anti-Judaistic prejudices of Christianity. The perception of the "enemies of the nation" did not move in the direction of modern anti-Semitism, and did not seek enemies within the nation.

The power of this relationship is demonstrated in the 1870s by the formation of anti-Semitic parties which defined themselves by the image of the internal enemy.[14] The reformulated national awareness

not only gave preference to the ethnic dimension, it attempted to enforce an exclusive link between the concepts of "Hungarian" and "Christian"—in the religious rather than the cultural sense. Jews were thus presented as an internal enemy, a group that had somehow "wormed their way into" the healthy national body and were rotting it from within. It was thus permissible to restrict their social opportunities and liberties, and beneficial to expel and remove them. Linking Christianity and Hungarian identity removed the concept of undivided liberty from the Hungarian ideal.

The Hungarian political elite of the time rejected both anti-Semitism and its political party. This was not just because it suited their interests to do so; they had become socialized by, and thought in terms of, the standards of the nation concept adopted in 1848–49.

However, none of this could remove the narrowed interpretation of the nation, or prevent it gaining new force in the mid-1890s with the formation of the Catholic People's Party.[15] What drove the ideals and organization of the Catholic People's Party was the struggle against separation of church and state. It conceived Magyar and Christian to be the same thing, and liberal developments (such as the ecclesiastical policy acts) to be destroying that link. It should be added that the separation of church and state was a long drawn-out process, urged by Ferenc Deák even in the 1870s, and was important for reasons going beyond liberal dogma. The purpose was—as I have already mentioned—to minimize the significance of Catholic-Protestant antipathy and thus strengthen the power of cultural solidarity among Hungarians, who were themselves in a minority in the country.

A new situation arose by the turn of the nineteenth and twentieth centuries. Hungarians—partly through assimilation—found themselves in a majority in their own country. This did not stop the enormous accumulation—in the political arena and elsewhere—of societal-national problems to which the power elite, by then incapable of correction or self-correction, had no answer. All that was left of their imagination and will was a clinging to the status quo. Put another way, the system had exhausted its internal energy and reserves by the 1890s. The problems accumulating behind the stability of the preserved status quo—the neglected societal implications of capitalization, the strengthening of national movements, the increasingly anachronistic operation of the

restricted franchise—opened the way for various radical movements and at the same time prompted the construction of a perceived internal enemy. The radical movements—regardless of their content—were primarily concerned with promoting sociopolitical identity, drawing the dividing line between good and bad to coincide with the division between themselves and others.[16] The traditional national consciousness could not compete with the ecstasy of seeking out internal enemies, and was therefore rendered increasingly hollow.

These problems were briefly covered up by World War I, only to break out with renewed vigor in the aftermath of defeat. The nation as a whole could be mobilized against the Russians, represented as enemies of the nation. The vision of national unity thus took on new life. As the country bled and limped its way towards defeat, there was an upsurge in forms of consciousness seeking to avoid its consequences by the panaceas: a radically revised concept of Hungarian identity, or class-based internationalism which might rise above such an identity.

But the consequences of defeat proved immune to any form of thinking or political experiment. Between 1918 and 1920, Hungarian politics tried out every form and identity hitherto developed in Europe, beginning with federative monarchy and ranging through republic, people's republic, and soviet republic, before settling on a kingdom without a king. Every one of these forms was accompanied by strong and mutually contradictory identities.

None of this made any difference to defeat and its consequences. In the end, this was what determined everything. Hungary had lost two thirds of its historical territory, and a third of people regarding themselves as Hungarian found themselves under the rule of other countries. Hungarians were in the overwhelming majority in what was left of the country, but their enemies had reaped an unprecedented triumph. The Habsburgs had become a thing of the past, but the former national minorities of the Hungarian state had come out victorious.

The trauma of the political elite was exacerbated by the events of 1918–19. The swings of power—especially the 1919 soviet republic—proved that even sections excluded by the former elite were capable of ruling the country. The leaders of the 1918 revolution and especially the 1919 commune included a great many people of Jewish origin. The inevitable message for the groups who had hitherto been in line for

power was that they must render repetition of such a challenge impossible once and for all, or face it again. The paradox was deepened by the fact that those achieving leading political positions were Jews in origin only, and not identity. Indeed they had consciously stepped out of the framework of Jewish identity, converting to Christianity or taking up a personal identity fully defined by communism. Jews who in every sense had spurned their Jewish origins found themselves interpreted as the group that embodied the essence if Jewishness. This was made possible by making origin, rather than identity, the focus of interpretation. Thus it was the experience of competition for power that moved the concept of Hungarianness in the direction of the racial interpretation.

This entire process was a traumatic experience for Hungarian national consciousness. The story of Hungarian nationalism suddenly appeared as a series of failures, and seemed to be in need of complete revision.

There were all kinds of proposals as to how it should be revised, but in practice only the version adopted by those in power could prevail. The counterrevolutionary system—which paradoxically came to power with the aid of Romanian arms—raised its own national consciousness to the level of state policy. In the interpretation of the new leaders, the catastrophe was caused by liberal politics; defeat was due to the inclusion of liberty in Hungarian national consciousness. They therefore preferred a restrictive version of national consciousness and an appropriately antiliberal attitude, drawing on the political conception of the Catholic People's Party and the Anti-Semitic Party. They saw their new conception as having two major virtues: it enabled them firstly to forge a link between the external and the internal enemies and secondly to create an internal enemy against whom they had a chance of winning. It was just the fillip that Hungarian nationalism—the least successful in the entire central European region—had been in need of. The conception obviously left no room for the realization that only the liberal national consciousness was capable of extending the existence of historical Hungary, and that no kind of national consciousness could have guaranteed the long-term survival of historic Hungary.[17]

Once in power, the counterrevolutionary system raised its conception of national consciousness into practical politics. Almost from the

beginning, it laid down discriminative legislation aimed at domestic Jews. Restrictive national consciousness, without respect for equality before the law, did not always operate in a straightforward manner. There were times when official discrimination was relaxed, but it always remained a guiding principle in social affairs. The coupling of Hungarianness and Christianity—rather than Hungarianness and liberty—always kept the logic of discrimination in operation. But it is also true that the system did not permit the ever-burgeoning racially-based concept of the nation to rise to the level of official policy until the 1930s.

This all applies to the "official" national consciousness. The original nineteenth century version of national identity did not completely disappear from Hungarian society, but it persisted only in a subordinate form, and with little political articulation.

The restrictive, racially-based version of Hungarian national consciousness received a strong international impetus with the victory of Nazism in Germany (1933). (A curious paradox of fate is that Gyula Gömbös, a prominent apostle of the racial idea and prime minister for a while, had German forebears, and another fanatic, Ferenc Szálasi, was of Armenian descent.)[18] National consciousness applying restrictions in religious terms lost its position of power, and racially-based, discriminative anti-Jewish legislation got under way in the late 1930s and went all the way to the Holocaust. The Jews no longer counted as Hungarians,[19] their opportunities were radically cut back and the redistribution of their wealth and possessions with a kind of socialistic fervour gave a large section of Hungarian society a direct interest in making a commitment to what was no longer a new national consciousness.

Now stripped of any idea of liberty, the racially-based Hungarian consciousness treated the widely divergent complex of Jewish identities, and identities of people who had renounced their Jewishness, as a single category. It then became irrelevant whether somebody was Orthodox, Neolog, converted, atheist, or any of the many other possibilities. They were just Jews, despite all the time thinking of themselves as Hungarians.

The state of Hungary betrayed a section of its own citizens. Its version of Hungarian consciousness debarred those who had "dropped into" Hungarian culture and the Hungarian nation-religion. The state, together with the concept of Hungarian identity it espoused, had forged

a new notion of Hungarian identity. Anti-Semitism, in the Hungarian case, thus proved to be a redefinition of the nation.

Standing against the reality of the disintegrated, fragmented Jews was a Hungarian national consciousness—now in a position of power—that adopted as its enemy, and thus as a fundamental part of itself, the total Jew concept. The narrative of the total Jew became a cold reality, viewed with incomprehension by most Jews, for whom it was completely irrelevant to their own identity.

Those who had assimilated had done so into a different Hungarian national consciousness. They cited their patriotic figures, their contribution to the elevation of the Hungarian nation, their propagation of culture, and many other things. But they were addressing a national consciousness that, although surviving at the social level, had lost its place in the realms of power. The new, racially motivated national consciousness, relegating equality before the law in the name of protection of the race, was simply deaf to the voice of the old Hungarian national consciousness. This deafness served its interests, and was an integral part of its self-definition.

The 1944 endgame cannot be blamed solely on the Nazi invasion. The essential mental and state preparations had already been made, and the racially-based, liberty-depriving Hungarian national consciousness was already in place. Years before the endgame, officialdom had spelled out what and how much could be taken away from the Jews, and had made it acceptable to take someone's rightful property and give it to someone else.

The Jews, clinging to the coordinates of traditional Hungarian national consciousness, reacted in the spirit of loyalty and respect for the law, and thereby deepened their own defenselessness, since nothing in their own articulated identity could have made them eligible for being regarded as enemies.[20]

The racially-based Hungarian national consciousness, depriving Jews of their rights, now perceived itself as an unalloyed triumph. The scope of life for Jews narrowed, they were deprived of everything that had been theirs, including, for many, life itself. Whether you were an Olympic champion, an eminent scholar of Hungarian literature, a great poet, or just a law-abiding citizen, now counted for little. Whoever you were, equality under the law was replaced by the equality of destruction.[21]

BEYOND JEWS AND HUNGARIANS— THE SPECTER OF COMMUNISM

The Holocaust brought unparalleled destruction. Some forms of Jewish identity lost much of their pre-genocide sociological weight within the Hungarian Jewish community through sheer physical elimination. Such was orthodoxy, which had been strong in some parts of the country outside Budapest. Since the vast majority of non-Budapest Jews were liquidated, it effectively vanished.[22]

At the same time, the Holocaust created a unifying experience for very diverse identities, a common history. This common history herded together those who had long been far apart from each other. It could also be said that whereas anti-Semitism could be lived with, got round, or got over, the Holocaust did not permit this avoidance behavior and attitude. The words of racially-based anti-Semitism became final and total acts, and the acts could not be ignored. In the logic of the events of the Holocaust, identity became worthless, giving way to an inexorable common history, and shared suffering.

Nonetheless, the Holocaust did not change the historical nature of the fragmented Jewish identity. At most, it altered the internal proportions. The anti-Semitic logic of the total Jew, even though it took the lives of hundreds of thousands in Hungary, did not come out victorious in the history of identity. Some Jews who survived, having in many cases lost their families, left the country and—out of conviction, need, or for emotional reasons—chose the Zionist solution, becoming Israelis. Some left the country for countries other than the newly-forming Israel. They could no longer live here, but that did not mean they broke from their Hungarian identities. The Neolog consciousness also remained, but its adherents were much reduced in number and dwindled even further under the later pressure of state secularization. Many also chose Christianity. And there also remained that other established route out of Jewishness, class-based identity. The latter also became spectacularly articulable, since the formation of the Communist system reduced or eliminated the opportunity for expressing other identities. The suppression and obscuration of alternative forms of consciousness was a special feature of the Communist system—one of the reasons it is referred to as a dictatorship—and was not restricted to Jewish self-

expression. This all meant that old self-definitions of Jewish identity as Hungarianness, in the forms of minor property owner, petit bourgeois or grand bourgeois, could not appear publicly, but they still existed and lived on in the ritual of private lives.

However, for those seeking a way to cast off their Jewishness, communist-socialist identity meant more than just another familiar option, even if it had already existed before the war. To abandon Jewishness was now an act supported and promoted by the authorities. It should be reemphasized here that a commitment to class-based and universal self-identification, if consistently pursued, meant abandoning any form of Jewish identity.

Taking such a step was influenced by both repulsion and attraction: repulsion from retaining any aspect of Jewishness and attraction to class-based Communist identity with its negligible national content. The repulsive forces fed on the weakness of existing bonds, the lack of comfort offered by Jewish spirituality for the radical stigmatization and disadvantage experienced during the Holocaust, the failure of any Hungarian form of Jewish identity to provide a relevant response, and the reduction of Jewishness in direct memory to no more than shared suffering. The attraction was that communism at least promised to overcome anti-Semitism, so that nobody would be suppressed, a new, fully-fledged identity, a kind of secular religion.[23]

The attraction of communism as a fully-fledged identity, a secular religion, was not confined to Jews of assorted backgrounds. But the motivation for post-Holocaust Jews to identify with communism stemmed from more than the promise that the Communist order would overcome anti-Semitism. What was on offer was a worldview in which anti-Semites themselves, and the perpetrators of the Holocaust themselves, were held up as the principal enemies. Nazis, fascists, whatever they were called, were fixed as the antithesis of Communist identity. Of course there were internal dissonances. The dissonances did not in the main derive from an identification of the strong similarities between Nazi and Communist methods and ways of thinking. The ideal of "class war" and the savagery of the war had obscured these, or at least made them subject to argument. The strength of emotional and political legitimization of the struggle against the "evil class enemy" and the Nazi brute proved powerful enough to keep the doubts at bay.

A much bigger problem was that in the model country of socialism, the Soviet Union, anti-Semitism had been incorporated into official policy. However, anti-Semitism was a much lesser part of socialist politics in Hungary than in the Soviet Union, and identity did not become so detached from experience, which is perhaps why the socio-psychological phenomenon of cognitive dissonance did not occur so strongly here. The conception that Communist identity held up anti-Semitism as the image of the enemy could thus be more or less sustained.

There was one factor, however, that made the choice of Communist identity easier for those who had a national identity, in this case a Hungarian national identity. Communism in Hungary—despite stereotypes to the contrary—set out to assert its power by means of vigorous national propaganda,[24] although the emphasis and strength of the national rhetoric changed its nature somewhat during the socialist period. It is undoubtedly true that the national worldview was highly selective, containing only what proved currently useful for socialist ideology. In general, two elements were highlighted: one was the "progressive" aspect of national history, and the other was the independence aspect. It might be summed up by saying that the more authoritarian the system became, the more it promoted insurgents as its precursors; the less independent the country, the more it touted the historical personalities of independence. However, the desire for identification was little moved by such paradoxes. After all, every religious worldview had always carried with it irresolvable contradictions. So now those Jews who had survived assimilation, had a Hungarian consciousness and naturally treated anti-Semitism as the enemy, became the potential and actual subjects of Communist identity.

People whose Jewishness retained a religious meaning or to whom middle-class lifestyle and personal property were important naturally enough regarded communism not so much an attraction as a development to keep their distance from.

The reaction of each individual was thus a combination of these repulsions and attractions. Some became Party members to avoid trouble, more as a "tribute" paid to the dictatorship than identification with it. With racially-based deportation out of the way, some nonetheless found themselves sitting on a train again, this time the victims of their class situation.[25] But there were some who adopted Communist identi-

ty with faith and identification, and it was a matter of chance, or the strength of character, whether they became propagandists of the new faith, or its inquisitors.

So it was not to avenge the Jews that they took this step but to escape from any kind of Jewishness, and find relief in a new identity. Vengeance for the Jews was out of the question in any case, because those retaining Jewish or Jewish-middle-class status were oppressed by the system just like everybody else. Either because they were religious or because they dared to show themselves as secular Jewish citizens.[26]

The anti-Semitic Hungarian national consciousness, avowing deprivation of rights, stated: it doesn't matter what you are—if I say you are a Jew, you are a Jew. Communism stressed: it doesn't matter what you are, if you are not a Communist, you cannot be anything else. Communism—in its aims, and for a while in practice—wanted to expunge and suppress any identities differing from it, thus forcing people into disguise or self-deception. It engendered fear, but offered a refuge from fear for those who joined it.

A large section of Jews, whatever kind of Jewish identity they adhered to, took the option of disguise. Do not talk about it, forget it, cover it up. It was something like an administratively-enforced assimilation.[27] But this applied equally to dissenting articulations of Hungarian national consciousness. As if national identity, at least formally, had dozed into some kind of "socialist patriotism."

And all the time, every identity that had entered the twentieth century was still there, sleeping, taking cover, being articulated only in the barest outlines, if at all. Life seemed to take its course along curious paths, with strange mythologies and countermythologies. From a student of a rabbinical seminary to a Communist, from a Communist to state security agent (AVO), from state security agent to a reformer within the system. Starting as a Jew, he found that everything that was Jewish had disappeared by the time he grew up. And the process sometimes went into reverse: from Jew to Communist and back to Jew again.[28] And of course there were those who lived here, beheld the specter of communism, and just wanted to survive.

ӾӾӾ

A large section of Jews converted to the secular nation-religion. They identified with it, but learned that the nation-religion had a many-faced god, and the church that took them in could also drive them out. Some remained loyal to their chosen identity,[29] some became disillusioned, and some sought a new faith. All of these variations occurred, and all are authentic, with good arguments to support them.

In the clear air of freedom, we discovered the existence of things we had never seen, and found many things whose existence we had assumed to be mere illusions. What seemed to have disappeared was here all the time, and what was here may no longer exist.

What is with us is the past, and the need to interpret it. And interpret we must, because we have to come to terms with everything that happened. Or if not come to terms, at least to understand, to get the past in proportion, and put it in its place.

We need all this to explain individual lives. To explain our utterances. To explain ourselves. Because we ourselves encompass identity history. Everything else is just a sketch.

Chapter Four

THE NEW JEWISH PAST

Assimilation, dissimilation, integration—three words of foreign origin expressing the opportunities in Hungary available to Jews in the full variety of their historical realization. Three paths to be followed, three ways of behaving, and three value judgements—and, of course, three possibilities of interpretation.

Assimilation began at the end of the eighteenth century and was primarily a feature of the "long nineteenth century." The basic question (or alternative) faced by Jews in Hungary and in other parts of the Habsburg realm in connection with their identity was: whom should they imitate and on what terms? Should they follow the notion of the enlightened and broad-minded ruler, Joseph II, and acquire a German-inspired dynastic identity to accompany the German names which they had been forced to assume? Or, in return for civil equality before the law, should they become Hungarians, accepting the offer of the 1830s and 1840s made by the Hungarian reform generation while its members were still in opposition? The years of 1848 and 1849 proved to be decisive for this question, as they were for so many others. Many of Hungary's Jews committed themselves to the national cause in the dispute between the dynasty and the Hungarians. They did so because they recognized the possibility of civil liberty for themselves, too. This was true even if formal equality before the law came too late and anti-Semitism, which was related to the fear of the loss of guild privileges, came too early.

The process was neither homogeneous nor without setbacks, but the trend became less and less questionable. It was no coincidence that Baron József Eötvös submitted a legislative bill concerning the emancipation of the Jews almost immediately after the Compromise. From 1840, Eötvös had been a consistent supporter of the offer made by the

Hungarian liberals. Nonetheless, Eötvös asked the Jews for something in return for legal equality; he wanted them to change their religious culture and organization, which formed the basis of their detachment and isolation. (We should add that—for other reasons, but with the same goal of bourgeois development in mind—Eötvös also wanted to change the Catholic organizing principles which lay at the root of the feudalistic perspective of the world.) A part of the Jewish population was prepared to do this; Jews belonging to this group established their own so-called organization "Neolog" (Reform), even though this led to a split in their community. The Neologs became increasingly dominant over time. Jews also developed patterns of behavior which were more secular and more in keeping with their new lifestyle.

These developments, which occurred at the level of the legal, political and ecclesiastical elite, would have been of little validity if they had not been supported by real changes in society. Increasing numbers of Jews in Hungary regarded Hungarian as their first language; more and more Jews were actively involved in the economic and political system, and an increasing number of societal and social ties connected them with Hungarian society as a whole. It was precisely the success of the assimilation which led, by the 1870s and 1880s, to the development of a type of domestic political anti-Semitism which saw itself as a continuation of the anti-Judaism of the medieval period; it is for this reason that native varieties of ideas imported from medieval Europe made their appearance from time to time. The decisive stand taken by the liberal elite soon brought an end to the anti-Jewish hysteria. Nevertheless, the slogan for dissimilation—"Jews, leave our country!"—had been declared even if it was of little political weight. The renewed sudden outburst of anti-Semitism in Europe at the end of the century led to the establishment of the political formula or blueprint of dissimilation, i.e. Zionism, in the Monarchy, too. Although this political blueprint was also expressed by the Jewish side, in general Zionism enjoyed only limited and weak support among Jews. The formula was the brainchild of the upper middle-class intelligentsia. Still, it was from Jews belonging to the most backward and least bourgeois groups that supportive letters came in large numbers. This was hardly surprising given that the Jewish religion had received official recognition in Hungary (religio recepta) before the publication of Herzl's *Jewish State* and that the branch of

government concerned with cultural affairs in Hungary had decreed that children of Jewish religion were not required to go to school on Saturdays or on feast days. (The decree was reintroduced for a short period after World War II. Even present-day Hungary with all its democratic pretensions was unable to continue the 1893 ideas of Count Albin Csáky who was 'just' a liberal.) The challenge and answer of dissimilation became stronger between the two wars, and the late nineteenth-century ideas of Herzl, finding resonance among the survivors of the Holocaust, came to realization after 1945.

The logic of assimilation was justified and possible; it was also successful. The path of dissimilation was justified, possible, and successful in a later phase. However, apart from some sporadic attempts, the logic of integration was not formulated with such strength as the other two during this period of assimilation and dissimilation. The main reason for this was presumably that the culture of integration was an immeasurably alien concept for national consciousness in each one of the east central European states. National consciousness—and here the Hungarian understanding of the nation was no exception—was developing on the basis of a logic developed against a background of threats and dangers. This meant that everywhere it strove for homogeneity. There was no possibility of equal treatment for Jewish culture or any other minority culture. Either individuals were Hungarian or they were not Hungarian; there was no room for different types of Hungarians, i.e., the conceptual idea of being Hungarian could not be reality and metaphor simultaneously. In the last century, Hungarian liberalism was also against multiple identity and cultural heterogeneity. It favored homogeneity, although it wanted to achieve such homogeneity through an extension of the law and equality before the law.

The Jews of Hungary also faced this dilemma and guarded against seeking the cultural modernization of their own identity, for they believed (with justification) that this would offer support to the anti-Judaic and anti-Semitic logic which disputed their equality before the law. And yet there clearly existed a graded and multifaceted process of integration given that the assimilation process itself was not completed overnight and that the secularized, but all-embracing, norms of Jewish religion led to the formation of a variety of subcultural groups. A logical and historical approach would suggest that the integration process

must have been present; but it was not articulated—it was without words. The mixture of sameness and difference in changing proportions was beset by the impossibility of definition, and it was this which led the individual to lie to himself and to the public. Often the person who chose assimilation overcompensated and became more Hungarian than the Hungarians. The "dissimilating" person (i.e., the person who chose dissimilation) behaved as if he had never had any particular bond to the culture; although it is quite possible that his real wish was to integrate—and this he would have done if the historical period and the way in which things were conceived had permitted. The concept of integration was a justified one and as a malter of policy was in the realm of possibility. Putting integration into practice, however, has hitherto always been denied and it is doubtful to what extent it could be successful now, among groups of well-entrenched assimilated and dissimilated Jews. At any rate, it seems that an attempt is underway now, at a time of perhaps more openness to the idea of integrative culture. Hungarian national consciousness, against a background of fundamental democratic rights, seem to be receptive to integration. The question is whether the past can tolerate this interpretative model projected onto history.

ӾӾӾ

The themes of the following analysis are based on Kinga Frojimovics, Géza Komoróczy, Viktória Pusztai, Andrea Strbik, *A zsidó Budapest. Emlékek, szertártasok, történelem* [Jewish Budapest. Monuments, Rites, History] (Budapest: MTA Judaisztikai Kutatócsoport, 1995), vols. 1–2.

HOW SHOULD WE CALL THEM?

After World War I, in the first anti-Semitic hate campaigns, they started to mention the original German-Jewish form of the name in addition to the Hungarian. This was done as an insult or in an attempt to exclude the person from Hungarian public life (vol. 1, p. 289).

Alfréd Hajós (Guttmann) (1875–1955), as an architect...(vol. 2, p. 462).

In my judgement, we historians proceed correctly if we call people as they called themselves—supposing that we do indeed know the name which they used for themselves. Of course, in case where the person changed his name, we have to say what his name had been—we can include it somewhere in the text about him. The use of both (Hungarian and German) names is not justified; people presumably changed their names because they did not wish to use the old one. Therefore, it is not surprising that use of both names carries with it overtones of anti-Semitism because naming people in such a way places their whole person in quotation marks and discredits them as individuals. Why use what we condemn in others? Why allow for ourselves what we evaluate negatively in others? The reason is obviously that it is precisely the contradiction posed by assimilation and dissimilation which the integration position aims to avoid. Therefore, integrationists must avoid the implicit anti-Semitism of using words in a way which casts doubt on the possibility of assimilation—even if they are aware of it. Naming people in this way is truly integrationist; but the price is high because it is ahistorical and can also be read as being anti-Semitic.

HOW SHOULD WE CONSIDER THEM?

The architect Béla Lajta was also a Jew. Nevertheless, he did not build the 'Parisiana' as a Jew. His job was that of an architect and he accomplished his task with modern tools and standards of art, style and taste (vol. 1, p. 327).

Most of those active in Budapest's entertainment industry were Jews....Yet most of them did not participate as Jews in their professions: they were artists, comedians...(vol. 2, p. 473).

This Budapest did not become "Jewish." It became "Hungarian." Contemporary public opinion considered and accepted it to be Hungarian...the question can be posed...what is Jewish in modern

> Budapest? But, given that those who established the modern city, with its buildings, spiritual life, atmosphere and character, were later called Jewish and simultaneously excluded from the community of Hungarians (excluded[?] exterminated is more accurate) by anti-Semitism and genocide, their work is also, retrospectively, classed as Jewish (vol. 2, p. 634).

Common sense and the requirements of qualification and talent in the modern division of labor dictate that it takes an architect to make a building; being Jewish alone is not enough. As an artist, a comedian working in the culture of a certain language—in this case the culture of the Hungarian language—is not a Jew but a comedian. Similarly, it is not relevant whether a tram driver is Evangelical or not, and a doctor's German extraction has neither relevance nor importance. Indeed, one of the most fundamental elements of the modern division of labor is that people participate in it through the exercising of learnable skills; other dimensions are of less significance. Of course, there are innumerable sociocultural factors determining the groups from which a certain profession will recruit. Nevertheless, once people are on their jobs the dominant role is played by their skill and their training. It is thus meaningless to state that Jewishness is the main factor in someone's design of a building. Here, professionalization is more important than origin.

Where is the meaning in this meaninglessness? It surely lies in the retrospective division of an assimilated culture into Jewish and non-Jewish elements which, instead of grappling with the historical-sociological points of selection, creates a kind of separate Jewish presence which is rationally and historically hard to justify. The pretext for this is admitted to be a feature of a later period: the backward projection of the racially anti-Semitic logic into the world of a public sphere which neither thought nor functioned in such terms. A Jewish identity adopted out of spite and turns out to be meaningless and ahistoric, and represents a kind of reversed projection of the racially anti-Semitic logic. Again, the imposition of integrative conceptual experiments on to the factual historical currents of assimilation and modernity is shown to be fraught with problems; we are in no position to tell people who were alive then that they planned buildings as Jews and not as engineers. Let us not look for a Jew where there is no "Jew."

HOW SHOULD WE DESCRIBE THINGS?

> The reservations of Orthodox Jews concerning the essence of the organizational changes of the Congress [of 1868–69] were justified. The alternative of modernization for the emerging Jewish middle-class was characteristically raised by the Christian state and not by a bourgeois or civil state: either equality of rights—in which case being Jewish meant the donning of a religious face only—or Jewish identity as a way of life—at considerable cost of isolation and without any real cultural modernization (vol. 1, p. 174).

> Yet the law [religio recepta] actually made the situation worse by permitting only clergymen (rabbis) who had received their training in Hungary to work....The Jews were turned into a kind of national church. A direct, if undesired, consequence of this was growing suspicion of every part of Jewish life which did not fit into the concept of religion. The recepció, for which the religious community had striven with all its might, ended up imposing Christian concepts of religion on Jews (vol. 2, pp. 351–352).

> ...under communist governments, József Eötvös's one-time liberal [emancipation] law provided the legislative framework for a purpose which was in complete contradiction to the original intention. Both the religious community of Budapest and the national organization...fell into a state of dependence; they became subordinates of the state administrative apparatus which directed the churches (vol. 1, p. 353).

Both the emancipation of 1867 and the reception law of 1895 took effect as dictates of a Christian, rather than a bourgeois state—and by a historical irony, even played into the hands of the communist state.

From here, we are not simply talking about the conceptual and historiographical problems of the integration logic; prejudiced and dehistoricized nonsense is at work. By designating religion as religion and, if possible, separating itself from the church, the state was engaging in a "Christian" act only inasmuch as the idea was the offspring of ancient Judaeo-Christian culture and was closely linked to the English and

French Enlightenment, and nineteenth-century liberalism. For the Jews, emancipation obviously meant the end of institutionalized anti-Judaism as well as equality before the law. It was thus a bourgeois rather than a "Christian" alternative, against which Orthodoxy, opposed to secularization, was (like the Catholic Church) only able to offer the maintenance of the old pre-bourgeois state of affairs. The fact that most Jews chose the strategy of adaptation rather than that of detachment was a rational solution and one which served their own interests, and there was absolutely nothing (except their own decision) to prevent their cultural modernization. The reception, which in Hungary occurred at the same time as the separation of church and state, did not impose the religious notions of Christianity on the Jews. Instead, it did no more than grant the Jewish religious community the same rights as those enjoyed by the other churches, which previously had been in a monopoly position. One could say that Jewish religion obtained legal status without anyone expecting it to make concessions on any religious matter. And, of course, the ecclesiastical policy disputes of the 1890s proved that the most aggrieved party of the legislation, which consisted of five separate laws, was the Catholic Church, which lost most of its feudal privileges. Indeed, in the eyes of the Hungarian state, religion became a private matter, a bourgeois development par excellence. It was no coincidence that, despite every efforts of Eötvös and Deák, it was these laws which were delayed longest; it was no coincidence that the pope displayed such antipathy; and it was no coincidence that the deeply religious Catholic ruler was so reluctant to approve them. Seen from this perspective, it seems even stranger that one of the most important breakthroughs of the contemporary bourgeois worldview and of domestic liberalism is described as simply a religious notion of Christianity. It is a meaningless, disproportionate view which seeks to cast as a failure what was the best thing that happened to the Jews during this period.

The devotion to folly seems to be endless; the emancipation law and (I think) the reception law—the latter sometimes being confused with the former—are portrayed (admittedly paradoxically) as having permitted the subjugation of the Jewish religious communities by the Communist dictatorship. Yet, how do equality of rights, reception, and the separation of church and state have in common with inequality

between religious and nonreligious citizens and the dictatorship of the state over the church?

Poor Eötvös!

There is only one explanation for such a mistake: the insistence on a Jewish world conceived in disregard of society and history, i.e., a world that does not and never has existed.

WHAT SHOULD WE DO WITH IT?

> The national assembly of 1839–1840...also considered changes in certain aspects of Jewish rituals desirable. For Jews the most acceptable of the proposals was use of the Hungarian language (vol. 1, p. 138).

> [Ballagi Mór] the great rabbinical expert, who nonetheless gave up his Jewish faith so that he could get a distinguished position and gain access to the Academy....The [Hungarian] Academy [of Sciences] had elected him corresponding member (1840)....In Germany he converted to the Lutheran faith (1843) (vol. 1, pp. 127–129).

> At the beginning of the 1850s, even the brave man Rabbi Lőw Schwab—who was held prisoner for a period of seven weeks from 17 August 1849 because he had held a service in accordance with a decree of the Pest city authorities on the occasion of the Hungarian Declaration of Independence (27 May 1849)—was in all probability cooperating with the Austrian authorities...(vol. 1, p. 141).

> In 1944, however, the religious community was simply unable to react appropriately to the situation (vol. 2, p. 353).
>
> Nonetheless, it is a fact that some Jews in Hungary—some Budapest Jews at least—although suffering terribly, did actually survive (vol. 2, p. 509).

The conceptual manageability of a Jewish integrationist position projected onto the past becomes especially delicate when this position

seeks to approach conflict situations—which occurred in the past and were different from those of today—according to its own order of values. In addition, the idea of an autonomous Jewish past in a period of strengthening interaction between Jews and non-Jews runs into further difficulties.

Jewish attempts at reform during the period of the Age of Reform cannot be discussed in isolation from contemporary developments in the country at large. If we wish to maintain the utopia of almost total autonomy, then use of the Hungarian language seems at best "acceptable." What are we talking about here? Under paragraph 8 of Act VI of 1840 on the Hungarian Language "only persons who speak Hungarian shall be employed in a religious function anywhere." The law regulated the use of the Hungarian language in numerous areas and preceded Act II of 1844 which extended these regulations. Thus in 1843 the Association of Becoming Hungarian [Magyarító Egylet] of the Jews was set up not because it was "acceptable" but because the laws of the land had turned knowledge of the Hungarian language into a condition for personal success and achievement. This was not an autonomous step taken by the Jews, but a recognition, once again, of their cultural, political and social interests—particularly those stemming from the greatly broadened rights afforded to Jews by Act XXIX of 1840. It is not possible to separate the history of the Jews from that of the state and public as a whole. Whenever we do this, we arrive at misleading concepts and false interpretations reflecting social conditions which never existed.

The situation is even more serious if we demand an exclusively autonomous Jewish image from individuals too. The conceptual deficit becomes quite simply prejudice. It is impermissible to claim that Mór Ballagi's conversion in 1843 was motivated by pure careerism just because he had wanted to become a member of the Hungarian Academy of Science three years before. We have no right to impose our conceptions on the fate of individual people; the consequences of such conduct is narrow-minded prejudice and idle formulations, a lapse of basic professional honesty.

Judgement of human behavior, its isolation from the historical context and, of course, the mixture of prejudice leads to uncertainty in other cases, too. In the case of "brave" Rabbi Lőw Schwab, a forgiving incomprehensibility surrounds the fact that he denounced the radical

democrat Ignaz Einhorn, who was known for his efforts to reform Jewish religion. Yet, Schwab cannot be regarded as a 'brave man' and it is nonsense to be "forgiving" of him. He was one of the leaders of a threatened minority who deferred to the Hungarian government when it was in control of Pest—a day after General Arthur Görgey took Buda—but wanted to score points with Alexander Bach when he took control. The rabbi was loyal to the government in power—and his means were not always admirable. The goal should be the understanding of behavior rather than the passing of moral judgement. Of course, this is only possible if we try to place historical actors in the events and context of their time and environment instead of separating them off from these. In other words, we are to do exactly the opposite of what is done in the passages quoted.

The utopia of an existence which is outside both history and society easily leads to a normative judgements of institutional as well as individual acts. An example of this is the "inappropriate" reaction of the Jewish religious community in 1944. Fifty years on, surveying the unmatched survival of a great many Budapest Jews and contrasting it with the great number of victims, who has the moral or historical right to pass judgement or give retrospective advice? Even the Israeli court presiding over the Kasztner case did not dare do that. Yet it seems that someone in the headquarters of the Alliance of the Jewish Communities of Hungary knows just what the "correct reaction" to the state apparatus of both Hungary and Germany would have been.

It requires great care to judge the dead. There should be more history and less big words—or indeed ideology. A little wisdom might also do some good, for the history of the Jews is especially full of dreadful situations to which there is no good answer. The arrogance of those still alive can cause only further harm.

HOW SHOULD WE VIEW IT?

> Is it possible in Hungary to lead a fully Jewish life without pressure to assimilate and be absorbed? As a Hebrew- or Yiddish-speaking Jewish Hungarian citizen, in other words as a Hungarian without limitations (vol. 2, p. 616)?

> Jews in the age of liberalism lived under the illusion that, through the struggle for emancipation, they had finally joined the family of European peoples. It seemed as if the ancient anti-Jewish feelings were gone for good and the Jewish community could take its place both in the state and in society as just another religious group. Since religion seemed to be the sole criterion of Jewish existence, many thought that agreement on religious principles constituted the unity of the Jewish community. But this agreement was lacking, and the Orthodox wings denied the existence of unity. Then the anti-Semitic movement started up in Berlin—a movement which would have denied political rights to all Jews without differentiation. Hungarian contemporaries joined the movement, led by Győző Istóczy. Hungarian Jews had opportunity enough and substantial reason to put their illusions aside. It is possible that the awakening sense of Jewish solidarity could have prevented the religious split; but the division was already an unalterable fact. It was only our generation which awoke, in the course of the final spread of the persecution of the Jews, to the fact that Jewish people, despite all their differences, share one fate /Jacob Katz, 1992/ (vol. 1, p. 175).

It is the main question (a very reasonable one) hanging over the integrationist argument: is it possible to live a fully Jewish life in Hungary free of pressure to assimilate? Here and not elsewhere. Of course we do not know the exact meaning of a "fully Jewish life" because—and from here the question stumbles historically—Yiddish or Hebrew are not usually the mother tongues of Hungary's Jewish population, which has already gone through assimilation. The question would have been absolutely relevant in the nineteenth century, had it been posed, which it was not. Any discussion of it now must take account of a social, historical, and cultural background which is much different from what prevailed then.

The problems of reasonable questions and incongruous, incompatible time frames have to be bridged somehow. This can be done by ideological historicizing if one has the appropriate predisposition. It is a predisposition which is itself a product of assimilation, for Hungarian culture is very fond of historicizing; a historical patina is often applied

to legitimize the often shabby and frail propositions of the present. The historicizing argument can therefore count on a reception; all that is needed is some substance. This demand is met by a train of thought which questions the reality of assimilation and treats real events as no more than illusions, linking the religious disputes going on within the Jewish community to modern anti-Semitism, a phenomenon clearly demonstrated by all research to have been rooted in economic and social discontent rather than religion. Then an unexpected turn. Retrospective and prospective proof, in the light of Nazi persecution, that the fate of the Jews is at all times and in all places indivisible. The arbitrary juggling of time frames and logical arguments once again denies the reality of Jewish assimilation, causing those Jews who took that route to appear as common idiots wallowing in illusion.

The integrationist logic is not made stronger by casting doubt on the historical validity of assimilation. And anyway, if we wish to expose the non-articulated projections of integration of that time, it seems that it is cultural and historical anthropology (daily life, family culture, etc.) which offer effective methods and contain the areas to be studied rather than a hopeless collision with emancipation and the religio recepta. Hopeless, because the alternative of emancipation was the absence of rights, and the alternative to the received religion. This had characterized the history of the Jews in Hungary for centuries, and I hardly believe that exclusion had filled the actors in that history with joy and satisfaction. It was no coincidence that when the opportunity arose their desire was for emancipation and for making Judaism a received religion. This was so because only these would grant them civil and human dignity. These men and women were no idiots; on the contrary, they proved to be people who saw things very clearly, and all the reprisals and tyrannies of the twentieth century were aimed precisely at the subjugation of the dignity and honor attained in the previous century.

Traditional methods do not appear able to deliver the historical projection of the integrationist argument—whose articulated form is peculiarly modern. The material is not really amenable to subsequently-formulated points of view, and the authors do not always look where they might find something. Their course of inquiry chooses to question the history of actual past events—instead of recognizing that the history of Hungary's Jews challenges the validity of neither assimilation nor dis-

similation nor integration. Each one, to a certain extent, requires its own methods, and for the integrationist logic, the past presents far more difficulties than the present. It is inclined to distort the past, for its function is more that of a new, hitherto unformulated Jewish interpretation than a standard historical explanation. History, in this case, is just an interpretation or a forgettable reality. The integrationist argument appears to face just as many difficulties as the assimilationist and dissimilationist interpretations, but of a different nature. The person who chooses assimilation—if he goes too far—loses his sense of being Jewish, and the person who opts for dissimilation is inclined to forget the cultural inter-activity of the Diaspora; integration—in its exaggerated form—can take on racist overtones.

HAS HISTORY DECIDED?

The magazine *Egyenlőség* promoted the rights and social acceptance of Hungary's Jews in Hungary, legal equality and the *Diaspora. Múlt és Jövő*, on the other hand, served to keep awake the idea of a Jewish homeland and state. Each of the magazines and tendencies had its own readers and followers. History, in the form of Hitler's National Socialist Germany and Hungary, did not deliver a just resolution of the dispute between the two camps, it simply decided the issue with tragic ruthlessness (vol. 1, p. 332).

No such decision has been made. Each logic continues to function; each one has had its successes and failures, and no one can be regarded as mad simply because they believe in one or another logic and organize their way of life accordingly. The history of the Jews cannot be written without the Holocaust; and Hitler has become a part of this history. But, even he was unable to make a decision. If the decision was indeed made by Nazism, this would mean Nazism had won.

It did not win.

CHAPTER FIVE

THE JEWISH CRITERION

THE PROBLEM

There much literature, both academic and nonacademic, in Hungary and internationally, proposing some kind of Jewish criterion or perspective. When I use the expression "Jewish criterion," I am talking about something that the authors, in their own interpretation, regard as a kind of guiding principle. They consider that such an approach exists and that it involves content and methodology by which it can be discussed, argued and admitted.

The Jewish criterion seems self-evident. It is not generally regarded or presented as problematic. If so many people say it, or take it for granted, then by this fact alone, it must exist.

I would like to subject this to some reexamination. Is there really such a thing? Does it exist in the way it is said to? And if it exists, what does it consist of? Maybe it does not. Maybe it is only something with no rational existence, just a proposed emotional reality raised to a concept. What is this Jewish criterion at all?

It may not be possible to give a clear and comprehensive all-embracing answer, but that, in my opinion, is all the more reason for thinking about it, because the search for an answer throws up other pertinent problems. If there is some kind of all-embracing Jewish criterion, then there must also be a Jewish essence, manifest in every—and every kind of—Jew. Is there such an essence, does Jewish essentialism exist? If so, then is it possible, for example, to write a common national history or common national literary history? Because if there is a Jewish essence then it must, by definition, always be different from the internal content of one nation or other.

As I seek an answer to this question, my thinking is of course constrained by a certain framework and certain assumptions. In other words, I have my limitations, which I should be frank about at the outset.

I am a historian, and so I approach the problem primarily in terms of history. I will not proceed in accordance with some theoretical, philosophical or religious-theological principle, or methodology. I know that these can give criteria valid in themselves, and where I see the need, I will indicate the importance of their potential and actual presence. I do not exclude them, but they do not occupy the main line of my thought. For example, although I must touch on the breakdown of the Jewish religion into various movements, I will not go into the differences of dogma and rules that divide such movements.

The historical approach will principally concern Hungarian history and Hungarian conditions. I do not, however, think this marks the limit of its validity. The assimilation of Jews in Hungary certainly differed from the Sephardic, where the community retained its own language and literature. Lessons from the Hungarian case do not really apply to Jews who did not undergo assimilation, or not to the same extent; for them the Jewish criterion is indeed valid.[1] For similar reasons, conclusions drawn from a historical discussion do not apply to the realities of a Jewish nation-state, for which national criteria are appropriate.[2] The criterion is also restrictive for a Jewish community whose declared historical logic and identity was and is expressly integrational, rather than assimilational. So the approach based on Hungarian history is also less relevant to the North American case.[3]

By contrast, Hungarian Jews, aside from some individual features, may be regarded as a model for every set of circumstances where Jews assimilated, where there was a strong tendency to secularization, where Jews were to some extent granted equality before the law, and where subsequently the Jews were collectively discriminated against by the state and then suffered the horror and reality of genocide. So as regards the problem of the Jewish criterion and its implicit questions and dilemmas, the Hungarian case goes beyond itself but has definite limitations. It is a difficulty for every historical approach that it can simultaneously be a model of wider applicability and have perceptible limitations. As such, it cannot reach the level of validity demanded for the logic of theories. On the other hand, theories often cannot handle the very historical processes (and associated theoretical problems) which they set out to interpret.

Difficulties are also caused for me by the language in which I am attempting to express my ideas. Not so much in combining grammar and vocabulary in accordance with the rules, although that can be hard enough. The real, and often intractable, linguistic problem is that a single expression can take on a diversity of meanings, sometimes not even overlapping. To take the Hungarian word for Jew (*zsidó*), historical stratification has charged it with constellations of content referring to religion, secular identity and cultural anthropology (in anti-Semitic, philo-Semitic and neutral senses) and can have a kind of spiritual content or sense from which the "body" is completely absent.[4]

I am not at all confident that I can achieve a satisfactory resolution of this conceptual-linguistic problem. All I can do is to set a context which hopefully delineates the interpretative dimension and, where there is a meaning I consider particularly important, to point out its implications. The question is further complicated by the emotional content attached to the word Jew, and the intense and understandable sensitivity deriving from reactions to the various narratives of anti-Semitism. This emotional perception can cause statements and discourses to be misunderstood. By taking pains with precision, this danger can be minimalized, but not avoided altogether. In endeavoring to express myself precisely, I sometimes find myself constrained to dry and certainly emotionless forms of words, although I would happily give rein to what little linguistic fantasy I possess, and there are some facts and phenomena central to my discussion in respect of which I cannot remain completely unemotional. I have strongly emotional and condemnatory feelings towards anti-Semitism and the Holocaust, but my search for a response is directed towards interpretation rather than declarations.

Besides these conceptual and emotional problems, and the limitations of applicability, there is another, comparatively minor difficulty: the different meanings generated by dissecting the validity and underlying content of the Jewish criterion in different time periods. It is an advantage of the historical approach that this issue can be resolved relatively easily. Nonetheless, time is an essential dimension in the analysis, for the primary reason that the Jewish criterion takes on intellectual relevance only on the breakup of the homogeneity that feudalism had given rise to among the Jewish people.

The issue dates from the time when the Christian worldview, pervaded with anti-Judaism, began to unravel, and the Jews—in both thought and deed—were able to step out of the ghetto they had been confined to. The Jews and their history had been homogenized through the operation of religious prejudices held by the state—although in a different way and phase—by the people. The state dealt more or less evenhandedly with its subjects of the Jewish religion, on whom the imposed restrictions acted as an external force holding them together and preventing any religious fragmentation or breakdown of solidarity.

When legal equality began, and the feudal exclusion ordinances of Jews disappeared, the homogeneity of the Jews also broke down. This went further than religion, so that secular and identity-policy inhomogeneities also appeared. The Jewish criterion, Jewish interpretation, Jewish essence arose in respect of what was actually an inhomogeneous medium, through the claims of society at large, antipathy towards the Jews, or even for claims for internal search for identity. The issue thus takes on substance—at least as regards Hungary—about a third or half way through the nineteenth century. The problem has been present ever since. All the more so because it was only after becoming utterly inhomogeneous in every aspect and sense that the Jews suffered completely homogeneous repression and genocide. So it could also be said that the truly problematic period for the Jewish criterion and the Jewish essence is what we might call the age of modernity. My discussion will therefore not extend to the anti-Judaistic regimes of the feudal age. I mention it as a point of reference, or rather as a starting point. Apparently a temporal restriction, this is actually a content boundary: the analysis is restricted to a particular time frame.

But even this is not enough. I would place yet another constraint on the validity of my own analysis. I am sure that the Jewish criterion and a whole set of related problems exist, and that these issues have only partly—if at all—received proper and consistent treatment. It is my conviction, however, that the Jews, having broken out of the feudal straitjacket, became inhomogeneous and opened up to more than one authentic definition of Jewishness. Diversity of definition also made it difficult—almost impossible—to come up with a universally-applicable reaction. That is perhaps why I have often detected some confusion when the Jewish criterion is mentioned and attempts are made to vali-

date it. Its relativity arises from the possibility of authenticity in different forms, of different and mutually contradictory interpretations. For example, it is possible to talk about the Jewish people in the general sense from the Zionist criterion, the Jews as a nation. Although some do not live in the Jewish nation state, the historical teleology of the nation concept implies that Israel is their proper place.[5] In this kind of interpretation, the Jewish criterion is obviously a national-ethnic viewpoint and this can even be authenticated for a period when there was not a trace of a national definition. This is an important example: a great many national interpretations apply such an interpretative schema and viewpoint to their own ethnic groups. Slovak, Ukrainian, or even German history and public thinking very often takes the now-established national viewpoint when interpreting a past in which the Slovak or Ukrainian nations, or the common German ideal, did not yet exist. This approach could be, and sometimes is, treated in a confrontational way or even completely rejected on the grounds of being ahistorical. However, by accepting the reasoning and argument behind different kinds of validity, one is prompted more to propose one's interpretation than to seek confrontation. Accordingly—although I will point out the internal and external limitations of some other approaches—my purpose here is to outline the problems and answers that have emerged out of my own logic. I am aware that competing answers and unmentioned identity-policy self-expressions also exist and that all of them have their own meaning, local value and indeed historical reasons.

Propositions formulated out of my own logic and vision are therefore not likely to remove or replace different visions generated in different minds. It is not my purpose to declare a non-existent unique truth, but to provoke conscious reflection on the problems I have put forward, reflection which may take a different form to my own. I would like everyone who is interested or concerned to be forced into giving an answer to the question: what really is the Jewish criterion?

ORIGIN AND IDENTITY

In European history up to the end of the feudal era, it was relatively easy to define who and what was Jewish. The expres-

sion, "end of the feudal era" naturally refers to different times, the story being much different in the Netherlands, than, say in Poland. The historical validity of different time periods, however, makes no difference to the fact that a Jew was regarded as someone whose religion was Judaism. This continued to be true even when the Jewish religious enlightenment reinterpreted many religious norms and brought a deep split among religious Jewish believers. The outside world looked on this as an internal affair of the Jews, and despite the spectacular phenomenon of religious inhomogeneity, Jews remained a single group in the eyes of Christian believers.[6] Although divided in dogma, the religion was still Judaism; Christendom could continue to interpret Jews in Judaistic terms and apply anti-Judaistic prejudices against them. This was enough to maintain the integrity of a concept of "Jew" which was otherwise beset by increasingly intense internal disputes.

In its anti-Judaistic thinking, the Christian feudal state usually treated the Jews as a unit and was even-handed in variously depriving them of their rights and restoring rights as conditions changed. A Jewish criterion for these circumstances—from the viewpoints of both the Jews and the Christian world around them—can be defined clearly and straightforwardly. There were, of course, exceptions even here, mostly individual, rich or cultured Jews, escaping the general rules. But these only proved and made more visible the rule that Jews as a whole were treated as a unit. It was possible to divest oneself of Jewishness and escape the conceptual and state coordinates dictated by anti-Judaism through adopting Christianity, since Christianity implied an identity in terms of religion rather than race or origin, and admission into it could, via a certain ritual process, be granted.[7]

Although this was quite common in other parts of Europe, it remained a somewhat sporadic phenomenon in Hungary for the main reason, in my view, that people drew greater security from within Jewish communities than they could expect if they ventured into the outside world. In addition to strong family and socialization mechanisms, oppression was not as severe as in Spanish territory or the papal domains.[8] So conversion was not typical, but it was a theoretical possibility. However, the anti-Judaism of the feudal world acted as a kind of external force keeping the Jews together despite religious schisms. There was a shared history and so there was, for this period, a Jewish

criterion. This gave Judaism an internal essence and anti-Judaism, deriving from the logic of fluctuating-strength state power, created an external viewpoint—a subject of possible research.

The arguable and definable existence of the Jewish criterion up to the end of the feudal era is not in question. Since the Christian state treated the Jews as a unitary whole, and the Jews effectively did not venture beyond the religious and cultural bounds of Judaism, there is no reason to question the complete validity of the Jewish criterion and the Jewish essence. The Jewish criterion, with a few individual exceptions, provides historical understanding of the Jews as a whole.

Intellectual interest in the problem stems from the ending of the ghetto existence which had been imposed from without by state policy and from within by the Judaistic community.[9] Secularization, professionalization, nation formation and the granting of equality under the law had the overall and combined effect of abolishing the constraints of the ghetto. These various processes did not all occur at the same time or with equal intensity, but their effects, whatever the mechanisms, were perceptible within one or two generations. The imaginary and actual walls of the ghetto were broken down from both within and without.

This situation rendered historically untenable the idea of a Jewish criterion embracing all Jews. Bonds to Judaism remained to varying degrees, but the overriding explanatory and identity-forming power of the Jewish criterion became open to question. In the process that generally bears the label "bourgeois development," new paths of social history and identity history opened up to people of Jewish origin, and this spelt the end of the Jewish essentialism which had held together Jews from within. As the common history behind it dissolved, Judaism assumed lesser importance.[10]

This "lesser importance" must be understood literally. Judaism became less determinant in everyday life; in people's thinking, its norms gave way to secular and professional norms and values; many people regarded as increasingly insignificant that which one or two generations before had dominated everything; and the rabbi was no longer the unquestionable source of wisdom for every Jew.

To maintain the exclusive applicability of the Jewish criterion, it had to be set about with intellectual provisos which ultimately relativized the viewpoint itself, together with its validity. The problems of

the outlook were well appreciated in the 1930s by Aladár Komlós, who attempted to survey the literary activity of Hungarian Jews in the nineteenth century. The weak point of what is otherwise an ambitious and well-executed work is his treatment of the Jewish criterion. He perceives the disappearance of the traditional Jewish criterion and essence—the generality of Judaism—but finds a single secure anchor point. "All that must be done is to survey every work originating from the pen of a Jew. These works, in order to avoid a sterile debate on the meaning of words, should not be referred to collectively as Jewish literature, but merely as the literature of the Jews." Thus only origin remains as a tangible and universal Jewish criterion. And the author himself realizes that this alone is not enough. He asserts that the purpose of his great intellectual enterprise is the "investigation of the process of assimilation."[11]

And there is the rub: if only origin counts, no meaning attaches to the identity-historical spectrum ranging from, say, an author of Judaic inspiration and subject matter to a conservative Hungarian writer, a spectrum in which every type stands closer to its own intellectual medium than to the community of its origin, a community in the process of dissolution.

"Origin" thus remains the only universal Jewish criterion, but has itself lost its universal meaning and significance. As an all-embracing Jewish criterion, origin has a role in more than the history of intellectual productions. For example, Lajos Venetianer, in his history of the Hungarian Jews from the time of Chieftain Árpád up to the end of the nineteenth century, published in 1922, largely applies the same criterion.[12] The origin criterion also worked in its own way until the nineteenth century, or at least half way through, since Jews and the cultural world of Judaism did not separate at any point, and the history of the Jews had a common level. From the second half of the nineteenth century, however, the origin criterion runs into just as many problems as in Aladár Komlós's cultural history essay. Common history and common essence cannot completely substitute for the religious circumstance of birth.

Many authors have attempted to apply the Jewish criterion, but I have mentioned these two works in particular because they are the definitive products of Jewish historiography and history of ideas from the interwar period, and stand out above all others. So if even the most

brilliant and thorough treatments—by the norms of the time—are so problematic as regards the Jewish criterion, then literature of lower intellectual standard must be even more so.

On the other hand, there was some foundation for an interpretation centred on origin instead of shared history and Judaism. It was intended as a vindication. The story of Jews becoming Hungarians, and thus enriching the culture into which they entered, was to be documented by the logic of assimilation rather than integration. This is an arguable position, and maybe borne out by the political norms of the time. But such a politically-motivated set of criteria, and the associated interpretation, do not satisfy the intellectual demand for proof of a universally-applicable, origin-based Jewish criterion couched in professional terms. Such a Jewish criterion can be explained historically, but is intellectually problematic, its argument being spoiled by an inability to accommodate the historical spectrum itself.

There was another consideration favoring the concept of origin, albeit without raising its validity. The definition of the Halachic laws of the Talmud of being Jewish—having a Jewish mother—enabled a section of Judaism to be preserved even in the secular world. This does not mean that the Jewish religion is based on race (although conversion involves a very complex procedure), but it was an important consideration. Neither should it be forgotten that state and church were not separated until the mid-1890s, and state statistics and population records kept account of each person's religion even up to the end of the 1940s. Interpretation on a birth-religion basis was thus technically workable, and could be used as a group-forming criterion without any extra research. The race-based anti-Jewish laws of the interwar period greatly broadened the database for the origin interpretation. It was almost self-suggesting and, as has been pointed out, seemed applicable on several interlinked criteria. It was also, or seemed to be, a good explanation for many things. It provided an interpretative framework in terms of sociology and division of labor and, with a bit of mysticism mixed in, could be used to prop up the "Jewish essence," which had otherwise lost its universality.

It goes without saying that the origin-based Jewish criterion was adopted by the anti-Semitic discourse, with a somewhat different emphasis than the Venetianer or Komlós perspective.

Without going into a detailed discussion, I would like to make a brief reminder of the anti-Semitic viewpoint that developed in Hungary and elsewhere from the 1870s onwards. The "total Jew" concept took shape when ghetto Jewry, common Jewish history, and the unchallenged, all-embracing dominance of Judaism all started to dissolve. Fundamental to the anti-Semitic view was that whoever is born a Jew remains Jewish in life, profession and identity. If we do not perceive the total Jewishness of such a person, that is only because he/she is cleverly disguising it. After the relaxation of the social confinement that had held the Jews together, the anti-Semites created the myth of unfathomable solidarity sustained by Jews in every circumstance—visibly and invisibly—with the purpose establishing total domination by the total Jew. As it gradually shifted its argument from "origin" to "race," anti-Semitism created a construct which could be deployed, via a movement and a doctrine, to defy real historical, cultural and societal processes. What was at stake was the possibility of revoking legal equality for Jews, or to put it in "postmodern" terms, the possibility of fashioning anti-Jewish practices out of the construct.

There were even some staunch anti-Semites who realized that the origin criterion could not cover the extreme diversity of behavior and identity. This realization was not a product of their intelligence or moderation. Tangible reality and direct experience simply showed them that the origin-race construction does not work as a universal Jewish essence, and cannot explain the manifestations of all people regarded as Jewish. The anti-Semite nevertheless retained his anti-Semitic conviction and voted for the anti-Jewish laws, but his experiences led to an intellectual expression of the existence of differences unexplainable on grounds of pure origin. In the debate in the Upper House of the Hungarian Parliament on the First Anti-Jewish Law of 1938, Reformed Church Bishop László Ravasz saw Jews as both a race and not a race, a historical situation, a historical feature, a "fabric of facts." He continued,

> So if the Jews form such a living organization, then we must also affirm that Jews in the territory of each nation present a different picture depending on how far their assimilation has proceeded. This is a long and varied road. There are advances and retreats, progress may be artificially held back, or promoted by education,

> but it is undoubtedly true that the process of assimilation has different phases which in particular cases generate and display different attitudes towards the national body and the national spirit. Owing to this constant assimilation process which is the, so to speak, ad intra movement of the Jews, it is an impossible endeavor to pronounce a final and universally-valid judgement on the Jews. The creature that is "Jewishness" is itself a dialectic. We therefore have to make mutually contradictory judgements to approach its nature....Someone can say that Jews are not Hungarian: whereupon they will put forward their soldiers of 1848, their heroic dead, their comradeship and courage in the trenches. Someone can say that Jews are Hungarian, and I have even heard that after the Reformed Church, Judaism is the most Hungarian denomination. Just board the train to Nyíregyháza and take a look in a third-class carriage carrying 60–70 Jews in kaftans and fur hats jabbering in Yiddish, and ask yourself: is this the Hungarian people, the people of [Chieftain] Árpád, the people of János Arany? (Applause and hurrahs.) The wandering Jewish Ahasverus puts down no roots, some have it; well, one could point to land-owning families of the Jewish faith who have been living in Transdanubia or between the Tisza and the Danube for a hundred or two hundred years, people whose land is their entire lives and the moral basis of their being, to which they are faithful and which they have served. So it is not possible to declare unilaterally one way or the other on the Jews. As it is unjust of the extreme right to seize on an individual at the beginnings of assimilation—and by assimilation I mean chiefly spiritual assimilation—and thereby to judge everybody who belongs to the fabric of this great diaspora, so it is a false defense for a Jewish person who is completely assimilated, a person completely adapted in spirit and morals, to demand on the grounds of his own case or that of someone in a similar position, for persons who are only at the beginning of assimilation, the same treatment which he himself deserves and which every just nation grants in respect and love.[13]

Bishop Ravasz was, I should repeat, an anti-Semite, and closed his speech with an expression of support for the anti-Jewish law. That his

experience had caused him, within his own logic, to appreciate the injustice of the act, and that he knew full well the severe pain it would cause, only aggravates his moral position. There is nothing to exonerate Ravasz, but that is not the point here. What is important is that, despite intellectualizing its perceptions, anti-Semitism is incapable of treating "origin" as the essence of Jewishness, because it stuffs too many contradictions into the concept.

The bishop's words were fully consistent with the anti-Semitic course and discourse of the age and are of interest here as a good illustration of how assimilation had taken effect by that time, showing the peculiar tensions that can arise between intellectual perception and anti-Jewish state practice.

A politically acceptable response to this anti-Jewish construct of origin offered itself in the form of turning the origin criterion into a positive Jewish criterion. But whether applied in the negative or the positive sense, "origin" could not validly address the question of how a universal Jewish criterion could apply if there is no longer a common Jewish history. The anti-Semites constructed a somewhat disjointed common history and common essence, while the Jews, repudiating anti-Semitic logic, constructed another kind of common history and common essence. The reality was that nothing actually connected the convert Jewish-born minister of defense or the sculptor of national renown with the Nagyfuvaros Street rabbi or the peasant Jew.[14]

One would think that some kind of common Jewish history and common Jewish criterion might have emerged to challenge the political and intellectual articulation of anti-Semitism. Jews may have been less than enamored of anti-Semitism and its logic—although there were more than a few self-hating Jews from the late nineteenth or early twentieth century onwards, like Otto Weininger and Oszkár Jászi—but this was not enough to prompt a common Jewish essence. Firstly, the anti-Semitic worldview—at least in the Dual Monarchy period—did not become government policy. Its existence was palpable, but it was a construct without means, i.e. it did not dominate the power which could have enforced it—the state. Secondly, and based on sound arguments, it could be believed that assimilation and the achievement of equality before the law were becoming increasingly successful, and in the new conditions of free expression, all kinds of things were being said and

there was no need to take everything seriously. Thirdly, having broken out of the ghetto and progressively loosened their bonds with Judaism, people no longer thought of themselves as Jews in their language and culture, and so did not really understand why anti-Semitic thinking should apply to them.

Having structurally disintegrated in terms of identity history, Jews could not really follow the origin/race-based anti-Semitic logic even after it reached the level of state power, and could not grasp the qualitatively new situation in which they were regarded—by external criteria—as a homogeneous body and their legal position and even their life were under threat. A good illustration of this peculiar narrowness of thought is a converzation which took place when congregational leader Samu Stern and three Jewish members of the Upper House of parliament went to meet Regent Miklós Horthy in December 1937. The intellectual and political medium of the discourse was constrained by threat and total confusion. The regent made a constant distinction between Jews ("bad") and Hungarian Jews ("good"), and the Jewish participants equally consistently distanced themselves from Jews they also disapproved of.[15] And this was the time when—as every participant knew—living conditions for Jews were deteriorating and proposals for deprivations of unforeseeable outcome were in the air.

It was not because the participants were themselves subject to restrictions (although one or two may have been) that made this converzation so blinkered. What produced the confusion was the lack of an intellectual foothold to make sense of the political world. The constantly recurring criterion of origin, the only one available and an integral part of the contemporary discursive space, rendered incomprehensible the images and concepts that everyone involved derived from real life. Horthy knew that his converzation partners were not the objects of his own anti-Semitism, and the Jews, since they did not fit the views being expressed, presumed that the anti-Semitic logic was inapplicable to them and to many of their peers.

Another example illustrates how the origin and race viewpoint—by then raised to a means of state oppression—was too much to cope with for one's identity. More precisely, how the origin criterion clashed with the reality of identity history in which there was no longer an exclusive, all-embracing Jewish essence springing from within. The

following quotation may be somewhat long, but is justified by its importance. It was written by Miklós Radnóti, one of Hungary's outstanding poets and intellectuals of the twentieth century. The text was written in 1942 and is directed at Aladár Komlós, the man who, at about the same time, had written a Jewish-centric history of literature treating Jewish origin as a kind of essence. Radnóti had still not converted, but in terms of his worldview had long since regarded himself Catholic. The origin- and race-based state policy of the time naturally treated and oppressed him as a Jew. The text is a statement of identity which confronts the origin-centred "Jewish essence."

> How should I start....There are three "family pictures" on the wall of my room, three photographic reproductions. Barabás's copy of a somewhat unknown Arany painting, the head separately of the same painting, and the copy of a recently discovered Ferenc Simó painting of the elderly Kazinczy. Visitors not "in the know," nearly always ask of the Kazinczy picture, and quite a few of them of the Arany (not the publicly-known, folk-styled face), "your uncle?" or "a relative?" Yes, I reply, Arany and Kazinczy. And they really are my uncles or great uncles. My relations also include the convert Balassa, the Lutheran Berzsenyi and Petőfi, the Calvinist Kölcsey, the Catholic Vörösmarty and Babits, and the Jewish Ernő Szép and Milán Füst, to come a bit closer. And my ancestors? Berzsenyi saw with the same eyes as Horace, as did the Jewish Solomon, the psalmist King David, Isaiah or Jesus, Matthew and John, etc. I have lots of relations. But certainly not only Solomon, David, Isaiah, Ernő Szép or Füst! I have distant and close relations. I am sure this says nothing new to you. This is the way I feel and no laws can change this "internal reality."
>
> I have never denied my Jewishness, I am still "of the Jewish faith" (I will explain why later), but I do not feel Jewish, I was not raised in the religion, I have no need for it, I do not practice it; I consider race, bloodline, roots, and the autumn melancholy trembling in the nerves, all as bunkum and not the determinants of my "spirituality," "mentality," and "poetic ego." Even socially, I am only familiar with "the Jews" as a bogus community. These are my experiences. It may not be so, but this is how I feel and I can-

not live a lie. My Jewishness is an "existential problem," because it has been made so by circumstances, the laws, the world. It is a coerced problem. Otherwise I am a Hungarian poet, I have listed my relatives and I am not interested (only practically, in "life" terms) in the opinion of the current prime minister on the subject....They can reject me, accept me, but my "nation" does not shout down from the bookshelf, "move along, stinking Jew," the vistas of my homeland open before me, the bush does not entangle me any more than from anyone else, the tree does not lift its branches to stop me reaching the fruit. If I experienced such as that, I would kill myself, because I cannot live other than how I live, nor believe nor think differently than I do. I feel the same now, in 1942, after three months of labor service and fourteen days in punishment camp (and do not mock, I know you have been in the war, but that was different, it was not humiliating), excluded from literature, where poets hardly coming up to my ankles run free, a useless and unused teaching certificate in my pocket, even in the knowledge of the following days, months, and years. And if they kill me? It would make no difference. I am being slightly pathetic, I'm sorry, and this letter is going on and on, I feel I am saying nothing new to you and that we agree. Argue!

What would you take issue with? Yes, I know, I've got back to it. I do not feel Jewish. Why am I of the Jewish faith, then? I have nothing to do with religion, I only believe a tiny bit in the spirit-forming power of the race, etc., maybe not even that much. So it is difficult to explain, and to make it even more difficult, I will add that if I have something in common with any religion it is with Catholicism. Right at the start of my poetic career, when I was twenty-two, they confiscated my second book of verse, and I was prosecuted and convicted of blasphemy....That was when I resolved to convert, not to use the symbols of "another religion," because it is not "another" religion for me—the poetry of the New Testament is just as much mine as that of the Old, and I believe in Jesus too, I cannot think of a better word for it, although belief.... But then it became worse and worse to be a Jew, here and there the "change of religion" could have been to my advantage, and that made it ugly....So I stayed Jewish in religion too. But this has no

> bearing on my poetry. In the poetry of the convert István Vas, Jews have more of a role than in mine or in that of the Jew Zoltán Zelk. So I do not believe in either the "Jewish writer" or "Jewish literature." Reality, I am afraid, bears me out. Sometimes I look through the Jewish papers....Semi-talents and no-talents retreat into a warm little community, because they would not have withstood the free competition of writing even without the anti-Jewish law and 1942, and two or three brilliant poets and writers, for bread, dry bread and very little recognition. Because you have to serve there, and do what you are told....That is about my opinion of "Jewish literature."[16]

This long and somewhat confused quotation is a very good demonstration that not even the strongest external pressure is enough to create a homogeneous Jewish essence. And his declaration that he would not change his self-identity even if what he called a coerced "existential problem" was to kill him, is all the more convincing when we know that it ultimately did.

I do not, of course, think that Radnóti was expressing a generally-accepted or widespread form of identity. But that is just the point. We have no grounds for proposing that there existed any kind of generalized Jewish identity that could be straightforwardly derived from origin. If it is true that the all-embracing identity world of Judaism, constructed from within and embracing all of the Jews, had come to an end in the bourgeois assimilation process, then after that, identity must have settled into a new structure. Different elements of the structure could have involved different—and varying—numbers of people, but their combination showed that Jewish essentialism had ended; from then on, Judaism would be a point of identity for only a certain section. The internal Jewish criterion had lost its intellectual coherence and universal historical applicability: the internally-applicable Jewish criterion had decayed.

It had been replaced by Jewish origin, which both the Jewish and anti-Semitic sides had great difficulty in investing with universal explanatory power and a suitable range of interpretation and interpretability. The difficulty stemmed from the same reason as had caused the exclusive internal Jewish essence to disintegrate. Origin could provide a sociological handhold; it could be a relevant criterion in some cases and completely irrelevant in others. It could present the logic of

the discourse, but could not interpret its object through intellectual and historical explanation; it could not stretch the fact of origin to cover its message. It was not backed up by essentiality. It existed, and still does, but does not deliver what it promises.

COMMON SENSITIVITY

If bourgeois development, assimilation, secularization and professionalization had torn apart the traditional Jewish criterion (identity), then it also meant an end to the common Jewish history which had kept alive a community defining itself in Judaism. True, one might object, but what if the Jews, having divided up in this way, have a common history imposed on them? What if the Jews have a common fate regardless of the fact that there is no longer a common, all embracing Judaistic identity which has a strong effect on everyone?

This is certainly not a theoretical question, it actually happened. The Holocaust itself and the racial anti-Jewish laws created a common history for people who "in their own right" had less and less in common.

The Holocaust made Jews "total" through state policy, and applied the anti-Semitic origin criterion retrospectively over several generations. Having been rendered "total," Jews were then forced into a homogeneous situation by depriving them of their rights. First they were marked with a symbol, then concentrated geographically, and finally transported to their deaths. It proved impossible to exterminate the Hungarian Jews in the racial sense, but this was not through lack of trying as much as lack of means.

The anti-Jewish laws sooner or later caught up with everybody, but extermination was not meted out to everybody.[17] None of this takes anything away from the fact that several hundred thousand Hungarian Jews, and Jews living in Hungary, ranged across a very wide scale of identity, experienced common history of the Holocaust or the road leading towards it. The survivors also knew that if the Allies had not defeated Nazi Germany, then their turn would have come. It was not necessary to experience every element of the history to make it common.

But if there is a common history, then it seems there must be a Jewish criterion.

And I think such a criterion does indeed exist. But not one that can be compared to the internally-generated Jewish criterion of the medieval Judaistic world.

First of all, as I have already mentioned, the anti-Semitism adopted by the state took effect as an external imposition. It resulted in dreadful destruction, but could not "restore" the exclusive community of Judaism in respect of the survivors. Thus it could not repair the existing historical identity fragmentation, only change the emphasis of its structure. By this I mean that some identity groups were largely exterminated (Orthodoxy) and others were numerically expanded (like Zionist identity or adoption of Communism). Thus, in my view, the Holocaust did not create a Jewish community worldview turning towards Judaism, but left existing identities in place, with some shift of emphasis and structure. Part of this shift, of course, was caused by the oppression itself: a great many people either completely cut off their remaining religious attachments, or hid, suppressed or kept quiet about every link or potential link to Jewishness.[18]

On the other hand, the Holocaust became the only point of memory which linked up everybody—and I stress *everybody*—of Jewish origin. The Holocaust was, and remains, the only possible common point of memory. This common memory, despite its doubtless importance, does not make up for the fragmented identity and the lack of a common history built from within. It was a common history which, by virtue of its very absurdity, nobody wanted to continue. On the contrary, everybody who could, fled from it, which is one reason why it became difficult to talk about. The Holocaust is commonly shared Jewish history which no Jew ever wanted.

Among Jews long since inhomogeneous in terms of identity history, the powerful common memory and sense of shared danger created by the Holocaust took effect principally on cultural-political sensitivities. In its devastation, the Holocaust created a common memory and a common past for the survivors and their descendants, but did not create a universal Jewish identity built up from within. It gave rise to a common sensitivity rather than a common identity.

This common Jewish sensitivity, although not expressed as such, is not some abstract concept, but a living, tangible reality. Its lack of expression is logical, because if there is no common "internal" Jewish

history, then the sensitivity does not appear as an articulated common Jewish identity point. But it this common sensitivity that causes the Jewish memory, quite rightly, to prevent the slightest concession being made in respect of exonerating those responsible for the Holocaust or the road leading to it, or in respect of post-Holocaust anti-Semitism. This makes itself apparent when, in circumstances of democracy and freedom, certain historical figures and events come up for reassessment. The common memory created by the Holocaust was manifested when the proposal to erect a public statue to Pál Teleki, the Hungarian prime minister responsible for the race-based anti-Jewish laws, was judged unacceptable.[19] Also unacceptable is open or implicit anti-Semitism in public speech.[20] And naturally for the Jewish memory—regardless of identity—the Red Army's invasion of Hungary in 1945 remains a liberation, since the expression is the formula of Wehrmacht + Arrow Cross versus the Red Army, i.e. death versus life. Naturally, this does not mean that a memory point rightly fixed as a liberation can be extended to the period when there was no German military power and the Arrow Cross had been eliminated. This is when the Communist narrative breaks from the Jewish memory: for the former, the liberation meant the start and widening continuity of freedom; for the latter, liberation meant liberation but brought no common content in respect of the continuity of freedom. It resulted in security for some, but insecurity and oppression for others. Therefore, there is no common Jewish memory of continuity following 1945 or 1948.[21]

But even the general Jewish sensitivity arising from the Holocaust is not exclusive, since it goes beyond the Jews. The Holocaust is a watershed in attitudes to European values, and prompted a choice within European culture as a whole. The sensitivity of the Jews thus became part of postwar German culture, for example, and a constant point of reference for European politics and public speech. The narrative of total condemnation of the Holocaust and rejection of race-based deprivation of rights and discrimination became an axiomatic point of the main current of public speech in Europe. This does not mean that common Jewish sensitivity is not a self-contained part of the whole. The important point is that common sensitivity is not common history.

The Holocaust was, however, incapable of becoming a common point in forming the attitude of Jews to their assimilation. The post-Holo-

caust upsurge of the Zionist interpretation, driven by the very occurrence of the Holocaust, retrospectively challenged and attacked assimilation as a fatal error. This ahistorical approach looked at everything in the past through the spectacles of the intention to destroy the Jews. Others did not think this way, and did not arrive at any rejection of assimilation at any time. Both points of view can be argued, and both can be intellectually authenticated. I do not wish to set out the arguments here. I only want to point out that even the Holocaust was incapable of implementing a Jewish criterion that was completely homogeneous in itself and its application. The unwanted common history created a common memory, but not a uniform and universal common Jewish criterion. The common Jewish history imposed by total anti-Semitic practice lost its continuity when the imposition was removed. It left an ineffaceable impression, but did not create a continuing common history.

WHAT REMAINS—AND WHAT IS POSSIBLE

So where do we stand with the Jewish criterion now?

A broad debate about the existence of some Jewish essence implying a Jewish criterion—at least as applying to literature, that dominant area of intellectual production—last took place in Hungary at a conference held in 1997.[22] The speakers were generally uncertain in their answers, tending instead to formulate questions; in trying to map out "Jewish content" in Hungarian literature they actually opened up the whole problem. Although the continuing belief in a kind of "deep Jewish" essence and the persistence of an origin-centred viewpoint[23] were clearly stated, it was strikingly evident that the absolutism of origin is no longer viable.[24]

In the meantime, origin has continued to play the lead role in historical studies and related approaches, probably because of the availability of source material which is easier to handle and has limited explanatory power. Unfortunately, a historical approach artificially fitted into the priorities of the origin dimension renounces proper treatment of the problem I have covered here, one that literary history has perceived and is trying to interpret.[25]

As I have argued above, bourgeois development put an irrevocable end to the Jewishness that had existed in a duality of unchallenged

Judaism and ghetto life, and therefore broke down the Jewish criterion built out of this situation. Its successor, the origin approach, could not and cannot provide an intellectually valid framework—in either the Jewish or the anti-Semitic reading—for the social and identity history spectrum of Jews whose world of relatively uniform legal status and identity had disintegrated. The enforced narrative and enforced history—however horrific—could make up for the lack of a real all-embracing common history built from within by both individuals and communities.

Nonetheless, I do not believe that the lack of an all-embracing Jewish essence renders the concept of the Jewish criterion completely meaningless. I admit that origin can and does have interpretative power, especially at the beginning of the break-up of traditional Jewry. However, I believe that the further assimilation goes, the less is explained by origin. So origin is not an absolute, but a historically varying, criterion.

Secondly, I think that the external Jewish criterion, anti-Semitism, also exists and is capable of forming a common narrative and history unintended and undesirable from a Jewish point of view. This is also of varying power, depending on whether it "merely" exists within society or is raised to the level of state power, and on how far it gets. So it cannot be held as absolute either. Certainly it is a real and definable Jewish criterion, and most importantly, can be documented and researched with precision and historically mapped out, especially if it appears in state activity. And of course it is a possible basis for independent Jewish articulation too, and in a highly important dimension, since the Jewish criterion it gives rise to could generate assessments departing from the main national current and very much meriting expression in historical study—if any history was indeed being written with respect to such a Jewish criterion.

I would like just to make a brief indication of the different emphases that could arise in such a case. In the case of the Dualist era (1867–1918), Hungarian historiography now tends to the positive evaluation, but cannot completely dispense with strong and well-grounded points of criticism. But on the Jewish criterion mentioned above, the era of the Dual Monarchy is unambiguously positive, since state policy came out in favor of equality before the law for Jews and the legal reception of the Jewish religion, took action against anti-Semitic political behavior, and opened up relatively wide scope for free expression and choice of identity for Jews. As regards the interwar period, the main current of Hungarian his-

toriography is mainly critical, but admits some positive aspects. From the Jewish point of view, the Horthy era was a gradually unfolding tragedy, a period without the positive features of modern Hungarian history, in which the trend was towards deprivation of rights and narrowing of existential opportunities, ending with the death of several hundred thousand people who had first been deprived of their dignity, their rights, and their property.

I do not want to go further into the differences in emphasis that arise, because I am confining myself here to indicating the possible applicability of the problem and the criterion. It is certain that if historiography is based solidly on such a Jewish criterion, then the current practice of the universal national historical narrative will become untenable. But this criterion is also severely limited: it only applies where the state had a tangible policy towards Jews, whether that policy granted further rights or imposed religious or racial discrimination. In every other case—such as in the Communist era—this criterion cannot be exactly and professionally applied, because Jewishness was not a primary subject of state policy, which opens up the issue to partial arguments and subjective interpretations.

Thus even the origin-centred and state-centred external Jewish criterion is incapable of embracing the field of history in which modernity was providing what was most important, through the force of bourgeois development, or through socialism. This is none other than identity history, which is alone capable of grasping what made the Jewish essence and common Jewish history disappear. It is undoubtedly difficult to research, since each and every individual could be the subject of a separate investigation. It may be more easily handled structurally, although it would be almost impossible to establish quantifiable backing for the structural elements in the statistical and sociological sense. It is nonetheless important, because it documents the limitations of the origin interpretation or the external Jewish criterion. Only identity history can reconstruct the actors of a formerly common, and then disintegrating, Jewish history not through ideological constructs, but in terms of the continuously experienced and changing world.

An application of the identity history approach gives a true appreciation of the relativity of criteria. We arrive at some perhaps strange-sounding propositions and conclusions, but the peculiarity arises only

because we are slaves to a paradigm that operates only within our own limitations.

If we regard identity history as being of major importance (and why should we not—understanding history means nothing else than understanding people who once lived), we can say, looking at how people regarded themselves, things like:

Miklós Radnóti (1909–1944) was born a Jew, and died for what he was born as, but he was not a Jew. He saw himself a Catholic Hungarian poet.

Oszkár Jászi (1875–1957) was of Jewish origin, received much anti-Semitic criticism, but converted and had nothing particular in common with any form of Jewishness. He was not a Jew.

Vilmos Vázsonyi (1868–1926) was born Weiszfeld, declared himself Hungarian, became a Hungarian minister and never broke from his Jewish identity. He was a Hungarian Jew.

Béla Kun (1886–1939) was Jewish-born, but his identity was internationalist Communist. Why would he be Jewish?

Vilmos Fraknói (1843–1924) came into the world as Frankl. He became a canon and then a titular bishop. Of course he was not Jewish.

Mór Ballagi (1815–1891), born Bloch, was a teacher at the Reformed [Calvinist] Church Theological Academy, and produced the first unabridged Hungarian dictionary. He was a Jew by origin, but a Protestant Hungarian by identity.

Max Simon Nordau (1849–1923) was born a Jew in Budapest, and almost became Hungarian, but then became French, and propagated the propaganda of the Jewish national idea. He was obviously Jewish. He had himself buried in the land of the future Israel.

Immánuel Lőw (1854–1944) was a rabbi in Szeged, a master of the Hungarian-language synagogue sermon. He was born a Jew, lived in the spirit of Judaism, was Hungarian, and died a Jew. So he was a Jew, but not in the same way as Nordau.

Baron Samu Hazai (1851–1942) was a Jew by origin, but was a Christian aristocrat and minister of defense, and a member of the Upper House of parliament from 1927. He was a Christian Hungarian general. Why should we consider him a Jew?[26]

From the point of view of identity history, these are still the simpler cases. There are much more complex stories. For example, the per-

son who is born a Jew, gains a Jewish identity, then rejects this identity, lives a large part of his active life otherwise, then in old age or just before death rediscovers his buried or forgotten Jewishness.

Whatever the story—and the story is almost impossible to uncover for the mass of society—it is impossible to ignore the freedom that the modern age affords people in choosing their identity, and thus deciding where they want to belong and which common history they want to become part of. Anybody considering himself/herself Jewish in some sense, is a Jew. If somebody does not consider himself/herself Jewish, we must be very cautious of our ground if we nevertheless regard him as "Jewish."[27] Because if we mechanically adopt "origin" in either the Jewish or the anti-Semitic interpretation, we are lumping together people who do not belong together on the basis of their own will, activity, or consciousness. And it is not by accident that they do not belong together, but by consequence of their conscious behavior.

So we must attach explicit qualifications to our criteria. The concept of the Jewish criterion cannot be regarded is universal and self-evident. I, as I have perhaps conveyed, am somewhat sceptical as regards the omnipotence of origin, and I do not think that either the anti-Semitic narrative that found expression in state power in the twentieth century or the Jewish equivalent, which in part was an answer to the anti-Semitic narrative, is a guide to use in investigating the history of identity of Jews who have become mutually dissociated. I think that our general criteria should be applied consistently with the actual dynamics of history, so that we simultaneously understand the explanatory power and the limitations of a criterion, or perhaps its narrowness and impracticability.

I am fully aware that the categories "Jewish non-Jew," "Jewish Jew" or "un-Jewish Jew" seem like linguistic-semantic absurdities, but such terms are necessary to apply the identity history criterion in an origin-centred semantic world.

This is no problem. The problem would be to consider as self-evident a criterion long since rejected by the very people it concerns. Our obsolete, one-track speech has been left behind by the experience of history.

NOTES

Note to Preface

1. The only essay being published here for the first time is *The Jewish Criterion.* The other four—in slightly different form—have already been published, "Zsidó utak—magyar keretek a XIX. században" [Jewish paths—Hungarian limits in the nineteenth century], *Kritika,* no. 1 (1992): 31–33, and no. 2 (1992): 25–26; "Miért nincs a zsidónak jussa a menyországban?" [Why don't Jews go to heaven?], in *Századvég,* no. 2 (1990): 204–211; " Új zsidó múlt" [New Jewish past], in *Holmi* 1, no. 9 (September 1999): 1300–1307; and "Zsidó, magyar, kommunista. Identitástörténeti vázlat" [Jewish, Hungarian, Communist. Identity history draft], in *A Komlós,* ed. Péter Kertész (Budapest: Ulpius-ház, 2002), pp. 440–467.

Notes to Chapter One

1. Pál Pándy, ed., "Lapok Petőfi Sándor naplójából" [Pages from the diaries of Sándor Petőfi], in *Petőfi Sándor összes művei* [The Complete Works of Sándor Petőfi] (Budapest: Szépirodalmi Könyvkiadó, 1955), pp. 445–446.

2. Mihály Vörösmarty, "Zsidóügy" [The Jewish question], in *Vörösmarty Mihály összes művei* [The Complete Works of Mihály Vörösmarty], vol. 16, *Publicisztikai írások* [Political Writings], ed. Andor Solt and Géza Fehér (Budapest: Akadémiai Kiadó, 1977), p. 80.

3. János Beér, ed., *Az 1848/49. évi népképviseleti országgyűlés* [The National Assembly of 1848–49] (Budapest: Akadémiai Kiadó, 1954), pp. 476–477.

4. Lajos Venetianer, *A magyar zsidóság története a honfoglalástól a világháború kitöréséig, különös tekintettel gazdasági és művelődési fejlődésére* [The History of the Hungarian Jews from the Conquest to the Outbreak of World War I, with Particular Regard to Economic and Cultural Development] (Budapest: Fővárosi Nyomda, 1922), p. 169. (In the writing of this chapter I also made use of the 1986 edition with an introduction by Tamás Raj.)

5. The speech on the emancipation of the Jews was delivered on 31 March 1840. The Eötvös essay dealing with emancipation was published in *Budapesti Szemle* 2 (1840): 110–156. Hereafter I shall quote from the version given in *Eötvös József Művei: Arcképek és programok* [Works of József Eötvös: Portraits and Programs], forword and commentary by István Fenyő (Budapest: Magyar Helikon, 1975), pp. 351–355.

6. Venetianer, *A magyar zsidóság története,* pp. 202–203. Recently, Ambrus Miskolczy devoted a small monograph to the problem of the 1849 emancipation. *A zsidóemancipáció Magyarországon 1849-ben* [Jewish Emancipation in Hungary 1849] (Budapest: Múlt és Jövő Kiadó, 1999), p. 11. The author of this substantial work refers to as "complex" what is interpreted here as the logical presence of liberal and antiliberal elements. The book is much more "understanding" and less critical than the viewpoint set out here.

7. Even the most eminent are susceptible to these, of course, as they are to attitudes arising from what might be called a mixture of ignorance and prejudice. So, for example, Vörösmarty writes in "Zsidóügy,"

> I should mention one more aspect. In the matter of the Christian and Jewish religions there is a meeting of East and West: the eternal rigidity of the East and the West's perpetually rejuvenating and serpentine nature do not allow us to doubt that progress and victory shall go to the latter. The rigidity of the East, with all its delights and familial license, cannot survive in places where the more universal and thus more humane freedoms of the West establish themselves, even only partially. The degraded faith and hypocrisy of the Christian West, despite all its debaucheries, at least maintains the pretense of a strict family life and thereby has a great advantage over the East, which delights in familial licentiousness, as a result

> of instilling in the hearts of parents the sacred duty of raising their children. Thus a more energetic, hardworking, educated and humane race is brought up which, besides inheriting similar principles and frailties and similar obligations, will always have an advantage over the races of Eastern upbringing.
>
> Is it possible for the adherents of Eastern religions to unite with a race of this kind without modification? Unquestionably it is not. The Eastern religious ceremonies and customs must be mitigated and either openly or clandestinely modified in order for this unification to take place. In this way, those Israelites [i. e., Jews] who have voluntarily renounced the outward features of their religion and its nonessential or defective regulations and principles have been able to join with the Christian community (p. 295).

When Vörösmarty puts forward "delight in familial licentiousness" as one of the main characteristics of Jewish Orthodoxy, he is clearly thinking of polygamy in Islam. This, of course, is immeasurably distant from the Jewish religion, and demands of the Jews something which Christianity had in fact adopted from them, not to mention the fact that the Orthodox view recognizes a fair number of obligatory regulations related to matrimony which do not always make possible the enjoyment of even one wife. The publication of such a patent error reveals more than just a gap in Vörösmarty's knowledge; it illustrates a widespread ignorance that must have been a factor in the formulation of demands for religious reform.

8. This act was nevertheless an enormous step forward for some Hungarian liberals from their position in the spring of 1848, when, in order to avoid the conflicts which threatened to split the Batthyány government, they even opposed popular representation in the counties. The 1849 law, among other things, accepted free language use in county assemblies, but still excluded languages of other nationalities at parliamentary level. (See András Gerő, "A magyar politika és a nemzetiségek 1848–1849-ben" [Hungary's policy on national minorities, 1848–49], *Társadalmi Szemle* 50, no. 6 (1987): 63–73.

There are two factors, however, which challenge the credibility of Kossuth's view. One is that it was formulated in emigration and not when in power: the 1848–49 nationalities policy was quite different.

The other is that, as news reached him from time to time, he redrafted the document to set varying limits to the freedom of national groups, depending on the extent he thought they would have to be involved in setting off a new struggle. The drafts are analyzed in, György Spira, *Kossuth és alkotmányterve* [Kossuth and His Draft Constitution] (Debrecen: Csokonai, 1989).

9. Lajos Kossuth, "Javaslat Magyarország jövő politikai szervezetét illetőleg, tekintettel a nemzetiségi kérdés megoldására" [Proposal concerning the future political structure of Hungary, with regard to the solution of the national minorities problem], in *Szemelvények az abszolutizmus kori és dualizmus kori magyar történeti forrásokból* (Budapest: Tankönyvkiadó, 1974), pp 14–33. Kossuth's espousal of integration set him distinctly apart from the vast majority of Hungarian liberals, and his opinion—particularly as it regards cultural autonomy—influenced subsequent Austrian social democracy.

10. "Act XVII of 1867," in Kálmán Csiky et al., eds., *Magyar törvénytár 1836–1868* [Hungarian Statute Book. Laws of 1836–1868] (Budapest: Franklin-Társulat, 1896).

11. The scale of immigration from Galicia had decreased in any case. (See Alajos Kovács, *A zsidóság térfoglalása Magyarországon* [The Settlement of the Jews in Hungary] (Budapest: Kovács, 1922). In the period following 1869, the number of Jews emigrating more often than not actually exceeded the number of imigrants. See Walter Pietsch, "A zsidók bevándorlása Galiciából" [Inmigration of the Jews from Galicia], *Valóság* 31, no. 11 (1988).

12. There is a substantial literature on assimilation. A few of the works I have drawn on are on the religious aspect: Gyula Zeke, "Szakadás után..." [After the split...], in *Hét évtized a hazai zsidóság életéből* [Seven Decades in the Lives of the Hungarian Jews], ed. Ferenc L. Lendvai et al. (Budapest: Magyar Tudományos Akadémia Filozófiai Intézet, 1990), part 1, pp. 145–161. The same book has statistical appendices on the assimilation process, pp. 185–197; Viktor Karády, "Zsidó identitás és asszimiláció Magyarországon" [Jewish identity and assimilation in Hungary], *Mozgó Világ*, no. 8 (1988); Karády, "A zsidóság polgárosodásának és modernizációjának főbb tényezői a magyar társadalomtörténetben" [Principal factors in the emancipation and modernization of the Jews in the history of Hungarian society], in *A zsidókérdésről* [The Jewish Ques-

tion], ed. György Litván et al. (Budapest: Velem, 1989); Litván, "Egyenlőtlen elmagyarosodás" [Unequal Hungarianization], *Századvég,* no. 2 (1990); William O. McCagg Jr., *A History of Habsburg Jews, 1670–1918* (Bloomington: Indiana University Press, 1989), pp. 123–139; and on the east European context: Róbert Simon, *Zsidókérdés Kelet- és Közép-Európában* [The Jewish Question in East and Central Europe], (Budapest: ELTE Állam- és Jogtudományi Kar, 1985).

13. See Judit Kubinszky, *Politikai antiszemitizmus Magyarországon (1875–1890)* [Political Anti-Semitism in Hungary (1875–1890)] (Budapest: Kossuth, 1976); György Szabad, "A polgári jogegyenlőség elleni támadás és kudarca" [The assault on civil equality and its failure], *Társadalmi Szemle* 45, nos. 8–9 (1982).

14. A reconstruction of the various views is provided in Zoltán Barotányi, "12 röpirat" [*12 pamphlets*], *Széchenyi Füzetek,* no. 5 (1992): pp. 2–39. "12 röpirat," a monthly journal of 40–45 pages (latterly 30) which came out between 1880 and 1892, was the mouthpiece of Hungarian political anti-Semitism. For a recent study on anti-Semitic violence, see Robert Nemes, "Hungary's Anti-Semitic Provinces: Violence and Ritual Murder in the 1880s," *Slavic Review* 66, no. 1 (Spring 2007): 20–44. I was considerably aided in interpreting anti-Semitic arguments by Kubinszky's book and György Szabad's essay. I also drew on: *Istóczy Győző országgyűlési beszédei, indítványai és törvényjavaslatai, 1872–1896* [The Parliamentary Speeches, Motions and Bills of Győző Istóczy, 1872–1896] (Budapest: n.p., 1904). Modern anti-Semitism, with some changes in terminology, manifests itself through similar constructs, and demonstrates no particular intellectual innovation. See the essays by Zsófia Mihancsik, Áron Monori, and Mihály Szilágyi-Gál, in *Antiszemita közbeszéd Magyarországon 2001-ben* [Anti-Semitic Talk in Hungary in 2001], ed. András Gerő, László Varga, and Mátyás Vince (Budapest, B'nai B'rith, 2002), pp. 63–110, and 121–130.

15. Stefan Zweig, *The World of Yesterday. An Autobiography* (Lincoln: University of Nebraska Press, 1964), pp. 102–104. Monographs on Herzl in Hungary, see József Patai, *Herzl* (Budapest: Pro-Palesztina, 1931); and Zoltán Halász, *Herzl* (Budapest: Magyar Világ, 1995). There is a wealth of international literature on Herzl. Notable among his biographers are Ruth Burstyn, Amos Elon, and József Fraenkel. The latest Hungarian book on Herzl is by Attila Novák,

Theodor Herzl (Budapest: Vince Kiadó, 2002). His work is largely a political biography and does not discuss analytically the identity history background against which Herzl might be defined, and in which his conflicts arose. The book is an addition to, rather than an extension of, the Herzl literature. By contrast, a major contribution to the identity history aspects of the story is by Gábor Schweitzer, who quotes Herzl as saying, "Hungarian Zionism can only be red, white, and green." See Gábor Scheitzer "Cionizmus a századelő Magyarországon" [Zionism in turn-of-the-century Hungary], in *Száz éves a cionista mozgalom* [A Hundred Years of Zionism], ed. Gyula Bódog (Budapest: Bethlen Square Oneg Sabbat Klub, 1998), pp. 41–51.

16. A good indication of this phenomenon and an attempt to treat it analytically is: Kati Vörös, "A Unique Contract. Interpretations of Modern Hungarian Jewish History," in *Jewish Studies at the Central European University*, vol. 3, *2002–2003*, ed. András Kovács and Eszter Andor (Budapest: CEU, 2003), pp. 229–258.

Notes to Chapter Two

1. Ágnes Kovács, ed., *Magyar Népmesekatalógus* [Hungarian Folk Tale Catalog] (Budapest: MTA Néprajzi Kutatócsoport, 1989), vol. 7/c, pp. 88–89, and 470–471.

2. István Széchenyi, in his book, *Lovakrul* [About Horses] (Pest: n.p., 1828], on horse breeding and horse racing argued fervently in favor of utilitarianism which was at the foundation of his philosophy. See András Gergely, *Széchenyi eszmerendszerének kialakulása* [The Formation of Széchenyi's Philosophy] (Budapest: Akadémiai Kiadó, 1972).

3. This quantity applies to the serf with private plot of land.

4. György Márkus, ed., *Brit moralisták a XVIII. században* [British Moralists in the 18th Century] (Budapest: Gondolat Kiadó, 1977), pp. 423–556, and 565–775. French moral philosophy Mária Ludassy, ed., *A francia felvilágosodás morálfilozófiája* [The Moral Philosophy of the French Enlightenment] (Budapest: Gondolat Kiadó, 1975), also deals with this question, but not with the same intensity as the British.

5. The most important literature as regards Hungary, in my view, is Ferenc Kölcsey's 1837 essay "Parainesis Kölcsey Kálmánhoz"

[Parainesis for Kálmán Kölcsey], in *Ferenc Kölcsey válogatott művei* [Selected Works], ed. István Fenyő (Budapest: Szépirodalmi Könyvkiadó, 1975), pp. 463–502), but many of Baron József Eötvös's essays and novels exerted strong morally-orienting force.

6. The historical context of this quotation is discussed in my essay, "Az iparfejlesztés kérdése a reformellenzék érvrendszerében" [The industrial development question in the arguments of the reform opposition], in *Nyolc tanulmány a XIX. századi magyar történet köréből* [Eight Essays on Nineteenth Century Hungarian History], ed. Csilla Csorba and András Gerő (Budapest: ELTE, 1978), pp. 111–162.

7. On the Védegylet [Protection Society], see Domokos Kosáry, *Kossuth és a Védegylet: A magyar nacionalizmus történetéhez* [Kossuth and the Védegylet: About the History of Hungarian Nationalism] (Budapest: Athenaeum, 1942); and János Veliky, "A kossuthi ipartámogató politika értelmezéséhez" [Kossuth's industrial support policy], in *Tanulmányok Kossuth Lajos politikai pályájáról* [Studies about the Political Career of Lajos Kossuth], Magyar Történeti Tanulmányok 9, ed. János Veliky (Debrecen, KLTE, 1979), vol. 11, pp. 67–90.

8. *Pesti Hírlap*, no. 150 (1842).

9. This problem is appreciated and analyzed in Lajos Mocsáry, *A magyar társasélet* [Hungarian Social Life] (Budapest: Müller Emili Könyvnyomdája, 1855).

10. This dilemma is dealt with in the play of Imre Madách, *A civilizátor: Komédia Arisztofánész modorában* [The Civilizer: Comedy in the Style of Aristophanes] (Budapest: Magyar Munkaközösség, 1938). It faithfully reflects the 1850s' dilemma of civilization versus Hungarian culture.

11. This issue is dealt with in Vera Bácskai, *Városok Magyarországon az iparosodás alatt* [Hungarian Towns during Industrialization] (Budapest, Osiris Kiadó, 2001), pp. 110–122; and Bácskai, "A pesti zsidóság a XIX. század első felében" [Pest Jews in the first half of the ninteenth century], in *Budapesti Negyed* 3, no. 8 (Summer 1995): 5–21.

12. It should be noted that military officers were not in the least overpaid. They had considerable social prestige, which they attempted to turn to their advantage in their marriage strategies, and were supported in this by the military leadership, which had to approve marriage and often only did so when the bride's family put down a deposit.

13. His route from frivolous cavalier to hard-working man of affairs is described in his diary: Frigyes Podmaniczky, *Egy régi gavallér emlékei. Válogatás a naplótöredékekből 1824–1887* [Memoirs of an Old Cavalier. Selection of Diary Fragments 1824–1887] (Budapest: Helikon, 1984).

14. Jenő Varga, *A magyar kartellek. Honnan származnak a milliók?* [The Hungarian Cartels. Where Do the Millions Originate from?] (Budapest: Népszava, 1912).

15. I refer to the cultural anthropological medium and not the social historical structure. There is a big difference. Whereas the former can be borne out at a thousand points—in my opinion irrefutably—the latter is the subject of debate and awaits proof or rejection. The thesis of a double social structure formulated by Ferenc Erdei, "A magyar társadalom a két háború között" [Hungarian society between the wars], *Valóság* 19, nos. 4–5 (1976), seemed capable of explaining many phenomena, and still does. It has exercised a major effect on historical study, as evidenced by several pieces by Péter Hanák and Miklós Szabó, for example. Viktor Karády is also a disciple of the double social structure thesis and it is partly via his views that Erdei's position was disputed by Gábor Gyáni, "Polgárosodás, mint zsidó identitás" [Bourgeois development as Jewish identity], *Buksz* 9, no. 3 (1997); and Gyáni, "Viszontválasz Karády Viktornak" [Reply to Viktor Karády], *Buksz* 10, no. 1 (1998). It is true that bourgeois development cannot be identified exclusively with Jews, especially as major groups of Jews effectively excluded themselves from the modern way of life on the basis of their values (to mention only the large number of Orthodox Jews, which have still not been properly researched). In addition, every non-Jewish centred research proves that bourgeois development had a highly diverse sociological background and mental orthography. I would mention three works: Károly Irinyi, *A politikai közgondolkodás és mentalitás változatai Debrecenben 1867–1918* [Versions of Political Thinking and Mentality in Debrecen 1867–1918] (Debrecen: University of Debrecen, Institute of History, 2002); Gyula Szakál, *Vállakozó győri polgárok 1870–1940. Sikeres történeti modellváltás* [Enterprising Győr Citizens 1870–1940. Successful Change of Historical Model] (Budapest: L'Harmattan, 2002); and Marcell Sebők, ed., *Sokszínű kapitalizmus: Pályaképek a magyar tőkés fejlődés aranykorából* [Multifaceted Capitalism: Careers in the Golden Age of Hungarian Capitalist Development] (Budapest: HVG Publishers,

2004). All these lines of research, some of them quite old, but nonetheless only recently achieving coherence, prove that bourgeois development ranged over a much wider scale than previously thought. On the other hand, an explanation is needed as to where the cultural-anthropological break point was, and why the view emerged among Jews that certain middle-class entrepreneurial values were associated with them from the time of the Age of Reform onwards, see Anna Szalai, ed., *Házalók, árendások, kocsmárosok, uzsorások. Zsidó ábrázolás a reformkori prózában* [Peddlers, Tenants, Publicans, Moneylenders. Portrayals of Jews in the Age of Reform Literature] (Budapest: Osiris Kiadó, 2002). There are question marks attaching to the "double" structure, but there is as yet no other interpretative answer.

16. According to urban Jewish "folklore," the difference between the pre-1918 era and Christian-national anti-Semitism was that before 1918, they said, "you're a Jew, but you're right", while in the Horthy era, they said, "you're right, but you're a Jew."

17. A thorough discussion of this in Dénes Némedi, *A népi szociográfia* [Populist Sociography] (Budapest: Gondolat, 1985). An anthology has been compiled—but not yet published—documenting the importance attached to the peasantry problem between the wars by the establishment itself. See Judit Bíró, ed., "Hivatalos falukutatók. Társadalompolitika és a vidéki Magyarország 1930–1940. Társadalompolitikai forrásgyűjtemény" [Official research into village life. Social policy and rural Hungary 1930–1940. Social policy source book] (manuscript).

Notes to Chapter Three

1. There is a substantial literature on this subject. For the most useful for appraising the background and the process, see Jacob Katz, *Out of the Ghetto: The Social Background of Jewish Emancipation, 1770–1870* (New York: Schocken Books, 1973). For Hungarian features, see Jacob Katz, *A House Divided: Orthodoxy and Schism in Nineteenth-Century Central European Jewry* (Hanover, NH: University Press, 1998).

2. For the wider historical context, see McCagg, *A History of the Habsburg Jews*. For a sketchier, but with a wider scope, see Nathaniel

Katzburg, *Fejezetek az újkori zsidó történelemből Magyarországon* [Chapters from Modern Jewish History in Hungary] (Budapest: Osiris, 1999). Originally published in Hebrew in 1975.

3. The developments of the Age of Reform are dealt with very subtly, via a particular area—education—by Viktória Bányai, "Zsidó oktatásügy Magyarországon 1780–1850" [Jewish education in Hungary 1780–1850] (PhD diss., ELTE, 2001). On the role of Hungarian national consciousness, András Gerő, "Zsidó utak és magyar keretek a XIX. században" [Jewish roads within Hungarian bounds in the nineteeth century], in *Magyar Polgárosodás* [Hungarian Embourgeoisement] (Budapest: Atlantisz, 1993), pp. 295–318. On the 1848–49 situation, Béla Bernstein, *A negyvennyolcas magyar szabadságharc és a zsidók* [The 1848 Hungarian War of Independence and the Jews] (1898; repr., Budapest: Múlt és Jövő, 1998); Jenő Zsoldos, ed., *1848–1849 a magyar zsidóság életében* [1848–1849 in the Life of the Hungarian Jews] (1898; repr., Budapest: Múlt és Jövő, 1998). For the fullest treatment of the emancipation, see Miskolczy, *A zsidó emancipáció Magyaroszágon 1849-ben.*

4. Viktor Karády has made the widest studies of Jewish secularization and modernization in recent years. His works have appeared in ever greater numbers. He mainly uses quantification methods. For his particularly useful work, see Viktor Karády, *Zsidóság és társadalmi egyenlőtlenségek 1867–1945* [Jews and social inequalities (1867–1945)] (Budapest: Replika, 2000).

5. For an understanding of turn-of-the-century affairs, see Péter Hanák, *The Garden and the Workshop. Essays on the Cultural History of Vienna and Budapest* (Princeton: Princeton University Press, 1998); Carl E. Schorske, *Fin-de-Siècle Vienna. Politics and Culture* (New York: Knopf, 1979); Steven Beller, *Vienna and the Jews 1867–1938. A Cultural History* (Cambridge: University Press, 1989); and Gábor Vermes, *István Tisza. The Liberal Vision and Conservative Statecraft of a Magyar Nationalist* (Boulder, CO: East European Monographs, 1985). The turn-of-the-century changes are treated by John W. Boyer's two monographs: *Political Radicalism in Late Imperial Vienna. Origins of the Christian Social Movement 1848–1897* [Chicago: The University of Chicago Press, 1981]; and *Culture and Political Crisis in Vienna. Christian Socialism in Power 1897–1918*

[Chicago: The University of Chicago Press, 1995]. See also Brigitte Hamann, *Hitler's Vienna: A Dictator's Apprenticeship* (New York: Oxford University Press, 1999).

6. These phenomena and the associated attitudes are well illustrated in Venetainer, *A magyar zsidóság története.*

7. For an attempt at a thorough review of anti-Semitism and its variations, see András Kovács, ed., *Az antiszemitizmus* [Anti-Semitism] (Budapest: Új Mandátum 2000).

8. The most easily accessible treatment in Hungarian is Halász, *Herzl.* It does not meet the criteria of an academic work, but gives a good account of how the originally assimilative consciousness transformed into a Jewish national outlook. See also Novák, *Herzl.*

9. The limits to the spread of Zionism are shown up by several approaches. To understand the limits of its influence, see András Kovács, ed. "Jews in Budapest," special issue, *Budapesti Negyed* 3, no. 2 (Summer 1995); and Géza Komoróczy ed., *Jewish Budapest: Monuments, Rites, History* (Budapest: CEU Press, 1999).

10. A good illustration of the attitude outlined here is the journal *Egyenlőség* [Equality]. See Lajos Szabolcsi, *Két emberöltő. Az* Egyenlőség *évtizedei 1881–1931. Emlékezések, dokumetumok* [Two Lifetimes. The Decades of *Equality* 1881–1931. Recollections and documents] (Budapest: HAS Centre for Jewish Studies, 1993).

11. I am referring to one of the most striking careers of assimilation of the age, and its conclusion: Henrik Marczali and his "affair." Henrik Marczali, *Emlékeim* [Memoirs] (Budapest: Múlt és Jövő, 2000); and Judit Bíró, "A Singer-Marcali ügy" [The Singer-Marczali Affair], in *Skandalum. Magyar közéleti botrányok 1843–1991* [Scandals in Hungarian Public Life 1843–1991], ed. András Gerő (Budapest: T-Twins, 1993), pp. 117–136.

12. There is an enormous number of sources and an extensive literature on the formation and character of Hungarian national consciousness. For the sake of simplicity, I mention here only one, which is both a treatment and a source, since it contains studies by greatest authorities and the words of contemporaries. The series published in 1998 by Új Mandátum Press under the title *Magyar Szabadelvűek* [Hungarian Liberals]. The twelve volumes give a thorough picture of liberal Hungarian national identity.

13. The mood of 48–49 is in my judgement best expressed by the first comprehensive treatment, whose author was also a participant. Mihály Horváth, *Magyarország függetlenségi harcának története* [The History of Hungary's Fight for Freedom in 1848 and 1849] (Geneva: Miklós Puky, 1865).

14. When I speak of the image of "internal enemy," I do not refer to evident social disaggreement. Social conflict, to a certain sense, is a continuous history of communities even when the modern concept of society evolved during the seventeenth and eighteenth centuries. Here I refer to the internal image of the "nation." For a study of the inti-Semitic parties, see Kubinszky, *Politikai antiszemitizmus Magyarországon.*

15. The Catholic People's Party, of considerable importance in understanding some utterances of the Horthy era—and some even nowadays—attracts relatively little attention from writers of Hungarian history. The best work in this area is a dissertation by Dániel Szabó, still in a manuscript form, to my knowledge. There are several references to the People's Party and its ideology in Miklós Szabó's political and historical essays, see Miklós Szabó, *Múmiák öröksége* [Legacy of the Mummies] (Budapest: Új Mandátum Könyvkiadó, 1995).

16. Social-based image of the enemy came to the forefront on both the left and the right. The logic that stamped the Social Democrats and the Radicals as "anti-national" was firstly an ideology setting out to overthrow the "class structure" and secondly a central element of the discourse.

17. On this, see Ignác Romsics, *Hungary in the Twentieth Century* (Budapest: Corvina, 1999). A slightly different emphasis is given in Jenő Gergely and Lajos Izsák, *A huszadik század története* [The History of the Twentieth Century] (Budapest: Pannonica, 2000).

18. Jenő Gergely, *Gömbös Gyula. Politikai pályakép* [Gyula Gömbös. Political Career] (Budapest: Vince, 2001); and László Karsai, "Ferenc Szálasi," in *Reformists and Radicals in Hungary*, ed. Ferenc Glatz (Budapest: Akadémiai Kiadó, 1990).

19. For documentation of racially-based legislation, see Róbert Vértes, ed., *Magyarországi zsidótörvények és rendeletek 1938–1945* [Jewish Laws and Decrees in Hungary 1938–1945] (Budapest: Polgár, 1997). Thanks are due here to Krisztián Ungváry for permitting me to

read his manuscript on the intellectual precedents to the expropriation of the Jews. For a contribution to the background thought to the legislation, see Ervin Csizmadia, *Makkai János* [János Makkai] (Budapest: Új Mandátum, 2001).

20. For a highly enlightening work as regards identity history, see Sándor Tibor, *Őrségváltás után. Zsidókérdés és filmpolitika 1938–1944* [After the Changing of the Guard. The Jewish Question and Film Policy 1938–1944] (Budapest: Hungarian Film Institute, 1997); Mária Schmidt, *Kollaboráció vagy kooperáció? A Budapesti Zsidó Tanács* [Collaboration or Cooperation? The Budapest Jewish Council] (Budapest: Minerva, 1990); and János Hoffman, *Ködkárpit. Egy zsidó polgár feljegyzései 1940–1944* [Curtain of Mist. Notes of a Jewish Citizen 1940–1944] (Szombathely: Önkormányzat, 2001).

21. The classic work on the subject is Randolph L. Braham, *The Politics of Genocide: the Holocaust in Hungary,* 2 vols. (New York: Columbia University Press, 1981). The question is put into a European context in László Karsai, *Holokauszt* [Holocaust] (Budapest: Pannonica, 2001).

I should note that the destruction of legal safeguards brought about by the policies of disenfranchisement and genocide, bathed as they were in anticommunist rhetoric, opened the way for the Communist policies of expropriation and deprivation of legal rights. There is an implicit reference to this in István Bibó's work, "The Jewish Question in Hungary after 1944," in *Democracy, Revolution, Self-Determination. Selected Writings,* ed. Károly Nagy (Boulder, CO: Social Science Monographs, 1991), pp. 295–310.

22. Unfortunately, for several reasons, the subject of the Hungarian Jews and Jewish identity in all its forms in the postwar period has been comparatively neglected. There are many blank spots and very little thorough research, although the political transition brought some welcome developments. On religious life and the intellectual life surrounding religion in the postwar period: László Csorba, "Izraelita felekezeti élet Magyarországon a vészkorszaktól a nyolcvanas évekig" [Jewish religious life in Hungary from the Holocaust to the nineteen eighties]; and Györgyi Tamási, "Zsidó szellemi élet Magyarországon 1945 után" [Jewish intellectual life in Hungary after 1945], in *Hét évtized a magyar zsidóság életében* [Seven Decades in the Life of the

Hungarian Jews], vols. 1–2 (Budapest: MTA Filozófiai Intézet, 1990). vol. 2, pp. 61–300. The other contributions in these books, covering earlier periods, are also well worth reading. János Gyurgyák's wide-ranging book, containing much data, *A zsidókérdés Magyarországon. Politikai eszmetörténet* [The Jewish Question in Hungary. The History of Political Concepts] (Budapest: Osiris, 2001), covers the post-1945 era only in the Epilogue. Tamás Ungvári, *"The Jewish Question" in Europe: The Case of Hungary* (Boulder, CO: Social Science Monographs, 2000), deals more with posttransition debates than post-1945 history.

23. Also not to be neglected are the instances of Jewish persecution even after the war. See, János Pelle, *Az utolsó vérvádak. Az etnikai gyűlölet és a politikai manipuláció kelet-európai történetéről* [The Last Blood Libels. The History of Ethnic Enmity and Political Manipulation in Eastern Europe] (Budapest: Pelikán, 1995).

24. I have dealt with this problem in another book. See András Gerő, *Az államosított forradalom. 1848 centenáriuma* [The Nationalized Revolution. The Centenary of 1848] (Budapest: Új Mandátum, 1998). For a summary in English, see Gerő, *Imagined History, Chapters from Nineteenth and Twentieth Century Symbolic Politics* (Boulder: East European Monographs, 2006).

25. In interesting view of this is given by the Gulyás brothers' documentary film on administrative exile during the Stalinist era.

26. The formation of secular Jewish consciousness merits study of its own, since both the secular socialist world and the resolutely anti-Israeli Communist propaganda were both involved in its creation. This form of Jewish identity became especially visible following the political transition, although its precedents had already appeared in the discourse, in urban folklore and in dedicated samizdat publications.

27. On these issues, see contributions by Ferenc Erős, András Kovács, Judit Mészáros, and Katalin Pető, in *Zsidóság, identitás, történelem* [Jewishness, Identity, History], ed. Mária M. Kovács, Yitzhak M. Kashti, and Ferenc Erős (Budapest: T-Twins, 1992). For another—literary—approach to the problem, see Iván Sanders, "Metakommunikáció haladóknak. Nádas Péter *Emlékiratok könyvé*nek zsidó olvasata" [Advanced metacommunication. The Jewish reading of Péter Nádas's *Book of Memories*], in *A határ és a határolt. Töprengések a*

magyar-zsidó irodalom létformáiról [The Boundary and the Bounded. Thoughts on Forms of Hungarian-Jewish Literature], ed. Petra Török (Budapest: National Rabbi Training Institute. Yahalom Jewish Cultural History Research Group, 1997).

28. In this sense, István Szabó's film *Sunshine* is pure history of identity. One of the strengths of the film is the demonstration that the horrors of Communism do not exonerate what gave rise to Communism.

29. A specific, but at the same time symbolic, example of hyperidentification is a grave at the Kozma Street Jewish Cemetery in Budapest. The inscription on the tombstone for a soldier who fell in World War I conveys the Hungarian irredentist spirit, since it is the revisionist "prayer" by Eleméрné Papp Váry, which was compulsorily read in schools during the Horthy era. The inscription on the tombstone of grave number twelve in the Heroes' Section is:

István Gyulay (died heroically in the World War I) 1891–1915.
On the east side of the tombstone:

> No, no, never ...!
>
> I believe in one God.
> I believe in one country
> I believe in a holy
> and eternal truth,
> I believe in the resurrection of Hungary!
> Amen.
>
> On the west side of the tombstone: brief Hebrew inscription

PETROGRAPH:
East side top: Hungarian crest with crown, map of Greater Hungary.
Bottom: shako, sword, lion's claws, palm and oak leaves.

My thanks to Vilmos Tóth, who put his collection at my disposal.

NOTES TO CHAPTER FIVE

1. On the Sephardic Jews and the problems of assimilation there, much different from in Hungary, see Heiko Haumann, *Geschichte der Ostjuden* (München: Deutscher Taschenbuch Verlag, 1990), pp. 92–164.

2. These national criteria are applied and outlined in Martin Gilbert, *Israel: A History* (New York: Morrow, 1998), pp. 5–37.

3. On this, see Arthur A. Goren, *The Politics and Public Culture of American Jews* (Bloomington: Indiana University Press, 1999), especially pp. 13–99. Things are different again in the Hispanic world and Latin America. An instructive case is Cuba, where those emigrating from North America counted as Yanks, and Jews migrating from the Ottoman Empire were known as "Turcos," just like the Arabs. After the turn of the twentieth century, many people who were not christened were regarded as Jews, including the Chinese. As a child in the nineteen thirties, Fidel Castro was known as a Jew because he was not christened. He himself was bewildered by this, because a "judio" in his homeland was a kind of bird. On this, see György Kukovecz, "Tranzitdiaszpóra (vázlatok a kubai zsidóságról)" [Transit diaspora (sketches on the Cuban Jews)], in *Zsidóság a hispán világban* [Jews in the Hispanic World], ed. Ádám Anderle (Szeged: SZTE Department of Hispanic Studies, 2004), pp. 151–174. The names and the Castro story are on pp. 156–157.

4. The history of "Jewish" as a symbolic expression and metaphor would require a separate wide-ranging analysis. In this regard see the wealth of data in Ungvári, *The "Jewish Question."* Many supplementary aspects are provided by Gyurgyák, *A zsidókérdés Magyarországon.* But since Ungvári is principally a literary historian, his work—although Gyurgyák works on a wider scale and his book is more comprehensive—is better focused on the symbolic category of Jewishness.

5. This concept is put forward in Samuel Ettinger, *A zsidó nép története. A modern kor: a 17. századtól napjainkig* [History of the Jewish People. The Modern Age: from the Seventeenth Century to the Present] (Budapest: Osiris, 2002). The book was originally published in Hebrew in 1969. In the period when their assimilation and secularization was taking place, the Jewish people, in the treatment of the author, were a dispersed unit, and their history converged in the foundation of the State of Israel (Israel is the structural frame of the work). The dias-

pora is thus measured against, and defined in relation to, Israel, and not interpreted on the basis of its own history. It is a relevant and arguable approach, but treats as unitary something that is actually highly fragmented. It also has difficulty in explaining why more Jews live outside than in Israel.

6. This remained the case even when the split in the Jewish religion led to irresolvable internal tensions. See Katz, *A House Divided.*

7. An instructive story is that of the Spanish converts. For an analytic work see István Szászdi Leon-Borja, "A converso Louis de Santángel," and an essay of Ádám Szászdi Nagy on the family background of Christopher Columbus, in *Zsidóság a hispán világban*, ed. Anderle, pp. 27–38, and 13–26.

8. On the anti-Semitism of the papal state, see David I. Kertzer, *The Popes against the Jews: The Vatican's Role in the Rise of Modern Anti-Semitism* (New York: Alfred A. Knopf, 2001), pp. 37–172.

9. For the classic treatment of this era that grasps this point perfectly, Katz, *Out of the Ghetto.* The social and religious aspects of the process are analyzed in Katz, *Tradition and Crisis: Jewish Society at the End of the Middle Ages* (New York: New York University Press, 1993).

10. Much local history research illustrates this process through changes in the social role of congregations and the Jews belonging to them. I would mention in particular Adolf Silberstein, *Hódmezővásárhelyi zsidók* [Hódmezővásárhely Jews] (Hódmezővásárhely: Hódmezővásárhely Izraelita Hitközség, 1943); Teréz Mézes, *Váradi zsidók* [Várad Jews] (Oradea: Literator, 1995), pp. 41–135; László Horváth, *A gyöngyösi zsidóság története* [The History of the Jews of Gyöngyös] (Gyöngyös: Mátra Museum, 1999); and József Ö. Kovács, *Zsidók a Duna-Tisza között. Társadalomtörténeti esettanulmányok, XVIII–XIX. század* [Jews between the Danube and the Tisza. Case Studies in Social History, Eighteenth and Nineteenth Centuries] (Kecskemét: Kecskeméti Lapok Kft. and Kecskemét Monográfia, 1996), pp. 105–223. All of the case studies show that the Jews no longer looked on each other as references, having integrated into the world hitherto regarded as "external." The increasing number of strands and relationships connecting them to this world broke the exclusivity of religious affinity. And if we include a source book and treatment of the interwar period (László Németh and Zoltán Paksy, *Együttélés és kirekesztés.*

Zsidók Zala megye társadalmában 1919–1945 [Coexistence and Exclusion. Jews in Zala County 1919–1945] (Zalaegerszeg: Zala Megyei Levéltár, 2004), we see—along with particular local features—a coherent picture emerging from local history research.

11. Aladár Komlós, *Magyar-zsidó szellemtörténet a reformkortól a holocaustig* [Hungarian Jewish Intellectual History from the Age of Reform to the Holocaust], vol. 1, *A magyar zsidóság irodalmi tevékenysége a XIX. században* [Literary Endeavors of Hungarian Jews in the 19th Century] (Budapest: Múlt és Jövő, 1992), pp. 8–9.

12. Venetianer, *A magyar zsidóság története.*

13. Henrik Fisch, ed., *Keresztény egyházfők felsőházi beszédei a zsidókérdésben* [Speeches in the Upper House by Christian Church Leaders on the Jewish Question] (Budapest: Neuwald Nyomda, 1947), pp. 32–34. This quotation from Ravasz's speech of 24 May 1938 is not taken from the parliamentary record. The editor, Henrik Fisch, was a rabbi in Kápolnásnyék, and published his book in 1947 with the inclusion of a photograph of his murdered daughter and a list of the twenty-three of his relatives who were killed. This was how he contextualized words uttered a good few years prior to the Holocaust. I quote from it, because I have no aversion to this contextualization. However, I would add a philological comment to Ravasz's words: when making a reference to an event that took place ninety years earlier, during the 1948–49 Hungarian War of Independence, he permits the inference that he had read or at least was aware of a book by Bernstein, *A negyvennyolcas magyar szabadságharc és a zsidók.*

14. The figure of the peasant Jew occurs in Charles Fenyvesi's memoir, *Mikor kerek volt a világ. Emlékek a szabolcsi szép időkből* [When the World was Round. Memories of the Good Times in Szabolcs] (Budapest: Európa, 1992). For the most recent discussion of this problem, see György Kövér "Performációk 1. 'Zsidó társadalom' Tiszaeszláron a nagy per előestéjén" [Case origins 1. "Jewish society" in Tiszaeszlár on the eve of the great trial], *Korall* 5, no. 17 (September 2004): 5–42.

15. Samu Stern, *Emlékirataim. Versenyfutás az idővel! A "zsidó tanács" működése a német megszállás és a nyilasuralom idején* [My Memoirs. Race against Time! The Operation of the "Jewish Council" during the German Occupation and the Arrow Cross Regime], (Budapest: Bábel, 2004), pp. 237–249. To convey the intellectual coordinates

of the conversation in an increasingly extreme anti-Semitic Hungarian political atmosphere—hardly a year before the first anti-Jewish law—I will quote a few passages. These also serve to illustrate that none of the participants in the conversation had any way of dealing with the overpowering force of the factor of ethnic origin:

> The regent mentioned that the raids are not directed against the Jews and that he was sure that the three members of the delegation were not in any way interested in that section of Jews who have infiltrated the country and carry out the abuses we are all familiar with. Turning to Stern, he said that perhaps the head of the congregation alone might have some concern for them on grounds of their faith. He went on to say that that 90 percent of the persons brought to account for the smuggling turned out to be such foreign Jews and only perhaps 10 percent were mailmen and suchlike from the lower orders, non-Jews in poor living circumstances who, perhaps for the purposes of treating sick members of their families, had offered assistance in the smuggling, which, since somebody's family is involved, is understandable on human grounds. But just as the regent did not identify himself with a person who, for example, when abroad, committed some unlawful act, even if the person was Hungarian and for example of the Reformed [Calvinist] faith, the same religion as the regent, he was sure that the members of the delegation did not wish to raise their voices in defense of hooligans and delinquents, even if they were Jews....
>
> The regent then said that in his youth he had been able to study very little Hungarian history. He was therefore somewhat unfamiliar with it; and what he could learn of Hungarian history in the occasional fifteen minutes at his disposal would not give a completely clear picture. He had a strong social sympathy, which cannot be said even of a ruler of such reputation and therefore popularity as King Matthias Corvinus, who lived in pomp, dressed himself in fine jewellery, and desired to be an emperor. He also talked of the time of Maria Theresa, who, according to him, had the right to rule Hungary alone, and so was merely queen of Hungary, because she was otherwise only the wife of Francis, who was later elected Holy Roman emperor. When the election took place, the

delegates of the electors gathering in Frankfurt did not include the Prussian, on the grounds that the city was occupied by Hungarian soldiers, and so the opportunity of free expression was denied.

After this diversion, he returned to the work of Hungarian Jews in developing industry. He mentioned that he had been at the Light Bulb Factory the day before, and what he had seen was in every sense magnificent. There were enormous exports of both light bulbs and radios. There was a great hall where radios made in the factory were packed for dispatch to England, Africa and even more distant countries, proving the genius of Hungarian industry; the company also had magnificent sporting facilities and every day the workers and administrators, to musical accompaniment, partook of excellent lunches of an abundance and taste to which even the regent was unaccustomed.

He mentioned that the company had a laboratory working on the development of a process which, if it comes to fruition, could short-change the company itself, because it would render the present manufacture of light bulbs unnecessary.

At this point in the regent's discourse, Vida interrupted to say that technicians of such genius were working in the laboratory that two young Jewish technicians had been invited to hold lectures in anti-Semitic Germany.

After Vida's intervention, the regent again stressed how much he esteemed the management and in general recalled the genius of Hungarian Jews with the warmest admiration.

That the world's film industry is in Jewish hands—Zukor and the rest—was denied by the regent, because Zukor was not a Jew, but a Hungarian Jew, and it is especially the Hungarian Jew who is rightly afforded the highest admiration across the world. It was no surprise that even in the field of fencing, a Hungarian Jew was the world champion, because he was no Jew, but a Hungarian Jew….

In carefully-phrased language, Stern declared that the official Jewish congregation felt absolutely no solidarity with "hooligans and delinquents" and those smugglers of which the regent had made mention in his speech, even if these were of the Jewish faith, and that there was no disagreement even in nuance among the other three members of the delegation and himself, the head of the

> congregation, in this respect. The official congregation never and in no way assumed any solidarity with this element and would never and in no way intervene on their behalf, indeed it was the official congregation which repudiated them most strongly and would not want this element to be defended at trial by outstanding Christian lawyer politicians; they should only be allowed and defended by the lawyer officially assigned by the court. The official congregation was aware that this element does the most harm to Hungarian Jews themselves, and thus does not support these people and disapproves intervention on their behalf.
>
> Stern's declaration apparently made a deep impression on the regent.

A regent who considered himself greater than King Matthias Corvinus and effused about the excellence of Hungarian Jews, and a Jewish congregation leader who partly distanced himself from the Jews—all part of Hungary in 1937.

16. Miklós Radnóti, *Napló* [Diary] (Budapest: Magvető, 1989), pp. 209–211. Radnóti actually converted on 2 May 1943 and murdered about a year and a half later. He was christened by Sándor Sík (1889–1963), who was of Jewish origin and became a Piarist monk.

17. The anti-Jewish laws gradually pervaded all walks of life. This is well—if not completely comprehensively—documented in Vértes, ed., *Magyarországi zsidótörvények*. The latest treatment of the process is by László Karsai, "A magyarországi zsidótörvények és rendeletek" [Jewish laws and ordinances in Hungary 1920–1944], *Századok*, no. 6 (2004): 1285–1304. On the Hungarian Holocaust, Karsai, *Holocaust* (Budapest: Pannonica, 2001), pp. 209–269. For the figures on death and survival, see Tamás Stark, *Zsidóság a vészkorszakban és a felszabadulás után (1939–1955)* [The Jews during the Holocaust and after Liberation (1939–1955)] (Budapest: HAS Institute of History, 1995).

18. András Kovács, "Identitás és etnicitás. Zsidó identitásproblémák a háború utáni Magyarországon" [Identity and ethnicity. Jewish identity problems in postwar Hungary], in *Zsidóság, identitás, történelem,* ed. Mária M. Kovács, Kashti, and Erős, pp. 97–113; and Barbara Hadházy and Zsófia Hamza, "Ahogy a 'másik' látja—avagy mit gondolnak egymásról és mit várnak el egymástól zsidók és nem zsidók

[How others see us—or what Jews and non-Jews think about and expect from each other], in András Kovács, ed., *Tanulmányok az antiszemitizmusról* [Essays on Anti-Semitism] (Budapest: ELTE Sociological Institute, 2001), pp. 99–120.

19. The contextual problems are reflected in the various articles in Ignác Romsics, ed. "Teleki Pálról fekete-fehéren" [About Pál Teleki in black and white], special issue, *Rubicon* 15, no. 2 (2004). On the history of the statue, see István Bakos and István Csicsey-Rónay, eds., *"Szobor vagyok de fáj minden tagom" Fehér könyv a Teleki-szoborról* ["I am a Statue but All My Parts Ache." White Book on the Teleki Statue] (Budapest: Occidental Press, 2004).

20. This is documented by the series *Antiszemita Közbeszéd* [Anti-Semitic Public Speech], of which I am among the editors. Three have already been published, by B'nai B'rith.

21. See Gyurgyák, *A zsidókérdés Magyarországon*, pp. 592–594.

22. Petra Török, ed., *A határ és a határolt. Töprengések a magyar zsidó irodalom létformáiról* [The Boundary and the Bounded. Contemplations on the Forms of Hungarian Jewish Literature] (Budapest: Yahalom Országos Rabbiképző Intézet, 1997). In her introduction to the conference proceedings, the editor precisely captures the arguments surrounding the issue:

> The entire discussion was haunted by the attempt to define a concept which could only be outlined in uncertain, and not at all in literary history terms. This is why the conference was concerned with the "boundary" and the "bounded." We could not say exactly which works and which writers were in our minds when we use the expression "Hungarian-Jewish literature": the extent of the interpretation—the "bounded"—is uncertain. So it is not particularly surprising that we do not know where the boundaries of this phenomenon lie, who/what might be parts of our system; and to which literary works and careers we can apply this expression (p. 7).

23. Miklós Szabolcsi discussed this and Béla Pomogáts disputed its foundation. In Török, ed. *A határ,* pp. 3–17, and 110–120.

24. Endre Kiss put forward very accurate observations on the issue of the relative validity of origin and György Haraszti also made an

excellent analysis of different Jewish identity versions. In Török, ed., *A határ,* pp. 23–36, and 271–283.

25. Many authors of Hungarian history—from local history to comparative and national history—have touched on the history of the Jews from various perspectives. The Holocaust research that has taken on such momentum over the last fifteen years or so has by its nature—and with full historical justification—given priority to the origin-centered approach. The same origin criterion—with far less reason—also dominates the study of other periods. Here, I should particularly mention the extensive research and many publications by Viktor Karády.

This author, who has produced much that is of value, has been little concerned with the history of identity. Taking origin to be absolute, he ascribes to Jewishness what should rather be ascribed to social position. Nonetheless, I regard his quantitative analyses to be very important, because *inter alia* they permit us to infer the significance of the identity politics factor, and the limitations of the origin-oriented quantitative approach now seem quite clear. In a certain sense, Karády has sensed the limitations of his own approach, as in his book of essays *Önazonosítás, sorsválsztás. A zsidó csoportazonosság történelmi alak-változásai Magyarországon* [Self-Identity, Choice of Fate. Historic Metamorphosis of Jewish Group Identity in Hungary] (Budapest: Új Mandátum, 2001), which still treats the problem mainly as one of quantification. He is, therefore, mainly presenting results of historical sociology and not identity history. This approach, in my view, shows that it is difficult to write the history of identity using quantification methods and results of historical sociology merely in a semblance. Overall, I consider that the origin-centred approach and the quantitative methodology have exhausted its intellectual energy and interpretative potential.

The problem is also sensed by Éva Kovács, *Felemás asszimiláció. A kassai zsidóság a két világháború között. 1918–1938* [Half-Hearted Assimilation. Jews in Kassa between the Two World Wars, 1918–1938] (Dunajska Streda: Fórum Minority Research Institute, 2004). An author who has produced incomparably less work than Karády, she proposes the importance of identity, but interprets it only as a problem of assimilation, a limitation probably related to the fact that, by her own admission, and as borne out by her monograph, she did not carry out a historical study. Her criticism therefore does not feed on a revelation of diverse historical

tensions, but is of an ideological nature, making wide use of the stigmatizing invective terminology of today's New Left. Thus Hungarian historiography is "writhing in an absolutist, colonialist (imperialist) trap of tradition." It is ethnocentric and nationalist (pp. 127–128). Collective stigmatization is problematic in itself. If we add to this that the author has no professional experience or appreciation of the results of products of the historical study, then there is even less reason to take her opinion seriously.

Otherwise, the viewpoint of historical study on ethnic origin appears in other, related areas and gives rise to very worthwhile results, although the Jewish content of the area under study is not at all clear. László Polgár, in his work *Shalom Haver. Zsidó származású magyar sakkozók antológiája* [Shalom My Friend. Anthology of Jewish-Born Hungarian Chess Players] (Budapest: Polgár Kft., 2004) reveals very accurately and interestingly the special problems that application of the origin criterion has created. The author writes:

> In gathering data, we came across surprising cases. One Jewish-born Hungarian grandmaster said of a chess master friend (the families had been close for decades), "I don't think he's Jewish." His wife picked up the telephone to ask their friend. It turned out, that their chess master friend was a religious Jew.
>
> Our work was hampered by the change of names in the second half of the last century, and by the names of non-Jewish fathers in mixed marriages. Furthermore, several Jewish chess players were buried in non-Jewish cemeteries (p. 32).

26. In producing this list, I used the relevant entries in Ágnes Kenyeres, ed., *Magyar életrajzi lexikon* [Hungarian Biographical Dictionary] 3 vols. (Budapest: Akadémiai Kiadó, 1967–1981); and Péter Újvári, ed., *Zsidó lexikon* [Jewish Encyclopaedia] (Budapest: Zsidó Lexikon, 1929).

27. This is also borne out by the defunct website *http://www.matula.hu*, where one was able to enter a name, and the website hosts provided information whether the person was Jewish or not. The basis of their definition was simple: whom they considered Jewish, was Jewish, regardless of the person's self-identity and origin.

BIOGRAPHICAL NOTES

Arany, János (1817–1882). Poet, schoolteacher 1851, secretary of the Hungarian Academy of Science 1865, and general secretary 1870–1879. His work covered the entire spectrum of poetry from lyric poetry and literary anecdotes to ballads, epic verses and major translations. Highly renowned in his own day.

Babits, Mihály (1883–1941). Poet, translator, short story writer, essayist, aesthete. Notable for lyric poetry espousing humanist ideals and often evoking the classics; was also active as a publisher, editor and promoter of talent.

Bach, Baron Alexander (1813–1893). Austrian politician. Interior minister 28 July 1849, effective leader of government 1852, and instrumental in Vienna's absolutist and centralist policy. Repealed the 1848 laws, but did not completely suppress the reforms of the Hungarian Revolution. The period 1849–1859 is known in Hungary as the Bach era.

Bajza, József (1804–1858). Critic, journalist, editor and poet. Leading figure in the literary world of the Age of Reform.

Balassa, Bálint (1554–1594). the first Hungarian lyric poet to take a place on the European stage, the great poet of the Hungarian Renaissance, the creator of Hungarian secular lyric poetry. His work combines love poetry with his experiences of the war with the Turks. Wounded by a cannonball at the siege of Esztergom, and later died of blood poisoning.

Ballagi, Mór (1815–1891). Theologist, linguist, dictionary editor, member of the Hungarian Academy of Science. At the request of József Eötvös, wrote the pamphlet *On the Jews* promoting emancipation. Took part in the 1848–49 Revolution and War of Independence. From 1855 to 1877 teacher in the Reformed [Calvinist] Theological Academy.

Barabás, Miklós (1810–1898). Painter and graphic artist. A favorite portrait painter, he painted or drew nearly every major person, politician, writer, actor, noble and haute-bourgeois of the time. Also known for his Biedermeier-inspired subject pieces and landscape aquarelles. He was instrumental in making Pest into an artistic center.

Batthyány, Count Lajos (1806–1849). Politician, prime minister of the first responsible Hungarian government in March 1848. After the revolution broke out, attempted to prevent armed conflict with the Habsburg empire, but judging his attempts to have failed, resigned in October 1848. Was involved in the war of independence and parliament. Taken prisoner in January 1849 and held in captivity before being executed for high treason in October 1849.

Bentham, Jeremy (1748–1832). English legal philosopher and economist. A founder of modern legal positivism. His works on jurisprudence produced the classic formulation of utilitarianism. He held utility to be the fundamental principle of social life, morals, and law; society should provide the greatest possible happiness to the greatest possible number of people.

Berzsenyi, Dániel (1776–1836). The great lyric poet of the period between the Enlightenment and the Romantic Age, and the outstanding master of classical verse. His early verses are reminiscent of Horace. His odes, together with an enthusiasm for nobility and the nation, embrace the main ideas of the Enlightenment. The crowning achievements of his lyrical art are his patriotic odes written in 1805–07 during the Napoleonic wars .

Bibó, István (1911–1979). Legal scholar, philosopher, professor. 1946–49: ministerial commissioner of the East European Institute, then chairman and leader. Forced out of public life after 1949, a representative of the "third road" in place of Soviet-type socialism or Western-type capitalism. Minister of state in the Imre Nagy government during the 1956 uprising, for which he was sentenced to prison from 1957 to 1963.

Bónis, Samu (1810–1879). Reforming politician, and government commissioner during the 1848 Revolution. After the surrender at Világos, he was sentenced to death, commuted to imprisonment, then released in 1856. Member of the "resolution" party in the

1861 parliament, and of the center-left after 1865. Retired from public life in 1869 to be a justice of the Supreme Court.

Castro, Fidel (1927–). Cuban politician. Involved in the left-wing student movement and was defense attorney in political cases. After an unsuccessful attempt to overthrow the dictator Fulgencio Batista in 1953, was sentenced to two years in prison. On release, went to Mexico, from where he returned to enter Havana at the head of a guerrilla army on 1 January 1959. First head of the armed forces, later prime minister. General secretary of the Cuban Communist Party since 1965.

Columbus, Christopher (c. 1451–1506). Genoa-born sailor and explorer. Hoped to reach Asia by going west. Refused support by the Portuguese king, he ultimately received what he needed—three fully-equipped ships—from the Spanish king and queen. Reached the continent of America (the island of San Salvador) in October 1492, and went on three further expeditions to the New World.

Csáky, Count Albin (1841–1912). Politician, minister. Member of the Liberal Party, follower of Kálmán Tisza. Minister of religion and education from 22 September 1888 to 10 June 1894. His so-called Baptism Decree of February 1890 set off the church policy dispute. President of the Upper House, 1900–1906 and 1910–1912.

Csengery, Antal (1822–1880). Reform politician, economist and historian, member of the centralist tendency of the reform opposition. Later, as a prominent member of the "literary Deák party," had a leading role in literary and academic life. A confidant of Deák, he was instrumental in setting up the Compromise. In 1868 Deák Party MP.

David (approx. 1040–970 BC). Second king of Israel approx. 1010–970 BC. According to legend, as a shepherd boy defeated Goliath, the Philistine giant, then secured the hand of King Saul's daughter. After Saul's death, became king of Judea and then all of Israel. Greatest figure of the ancient history of the Jews. The lyrical poetry of the Old Testament is ascribed to him.

Deák, Ferenc (1803–1876). Politician, legal philosopher, minister of justice in the first responsible Hungarian government, March–September 1848. In the period between the suppression of the revolution and the 1867 Compromise, he symbolized the legend

of "passive resistance" against Habsburg rule, and as member of parliament between 1861 and 1865, the leading figure of the Representation Party, the intellectual and legal author of the 1867 Compromise and its political representative. Following the establishment of the Dual Monarchy, he remained an MP but accepted no government post.

Dreyfus, Alfred (1859–1935). French army officer, subject of the Dreyfus Affair. In 1894, French intelligence accused him of spying on the basis of anti-Semitic prejudice, and a court martial sentenced him to life imprisonment. The affair severely divided public opinion, and a political dispute broke out with loud demonstrations and press battles. Rehabilitated in 1906.

Dux, Adolf (1822–1881). Journalist, translator, joined the staff of the *Wanderer* in Vienna in 1854 and the *Pester Lloyd* in Budapest in 1855. Propagated Hungarian culture in his German-language articles, and translated into German literary works by many contemporary writers and poets.

Dühring, Karl Eugen (1833–1921). German economist and anti-Semitic thinker. His works, above all *Die Judenfrage* [The Jewish Question], fervently attacked the Jews—and Christianity—as the manifestation of the Jewish spirit.

Eötvös, Baron József (1813–1871). Writer, poet, reform politician. In 1848 minister for religious affairs and education in the first responsible Hungarian ministry, minister for religious affairs and education from 1867 to 1871, responsible for the laws on elementary and compulsory education and on equal rights for Jews. His writing was a major step on the way to realism in Hungarian literarure.

Fraknói, Vilmos (1843–1924). Historian, canon and titular bishop. Produced a long series of essays on medieval and especially fifteenth and seventeenth century Hungarian history. He stressed the role of the church and diplomacy. He used many foreign sources, particularly from the Italian archives. He had a clerical-conservative perspective.

Füst, Milán (1888–1967). Writer and poet. His absolutely novel verse form and mode of expression was attacked from many sides. During the People's Republic of 1918–19, he set up the Associ-

ation of Artists and Scientists, and after the fall of the Hungarian Soviet Republic of 1919, he was the subject of disciplinary proceedings in his school. He was forced into hiding during the siege of Budapest in 1944–45. Became professor in 1948.

Gömbös, Gyula (1886–1936). Army officer, politician, prime minister 1932–1936. His domestic policy had elements of Italian Fascism.

Görgey, Arthur (1818–1916). Hungarian general and ministry of war. Became chief army commander on 30 March 1849. Following defeat at Temesvár [Timişoara], forced the government into resignation on 11 August, and seizing supreme power, surrendered unconditionally to the Russian forces at Világos on 13 August. Was pardoned during the period of reprisals. His role was long disputed among the public, in literature, and by historians, variously condemned as a traitor and upheld as a realistic politician.

Hajós, Alfréd (1878–1955). First two-time champion (in 100 and 1200 meter swimming) at the first Modern Olympic Games (Athens 1896). An outstanding architect, he is best knownfor the construction of the indoor swimming pool on Budapest's Margaret Island.

Hazai, Baron Samu (1851–1942). Army officer, minister of defense 1910–1917. From 1917 to the end of the war, was commander of the reserves of the common army. During the Horthy era, member of the board of directors of many banks and companies, and first president of the Hungarian Military Writers' Circle. Became member of the Upper House of parliament in 1927.

Herzl, Theodor (1860–1904). Journalist and founder of Zionism, which called for an independent Jewish state in the Palestine.

Hitler, Adolf (1889–1945). German politician, became chancellor in 1933, organizer and leader of the National Socialist Party, his violent expansionist policy and radical anti-Semitism led to the World War II and the Holocaust.

Horace (Quintus Horatius Flaccus) (65–8 BC). Roman poet, one of the great lyric poets of world literature.

Horn, Ede (1825–1875). Journalist, liberal politician and economist. Studied to be a rabbi. Jewish chaplain in the 1848–49 War of Independence. Emigrated after Világos, and wrote on economics. Returned in 1869, and became a member of parliament in

1870 in Kálmán Tisza's group. Became state secretary for trade in 1875. Extensive journalistic output, especially in exile.

Horthy, Miklós (1868–1957). Naval officer, regent of Hungary (a kingdom without a king), 1921–1944. His domestic and foreign policy was fundamentally determined by revisionism, the restoration of historic Hungary. After World War II, he lived in American captivity and then in Portugal.

Horváth, Mihály (1809–1878). Bishop, historian, cultural politician. Minister of education in the Bertalan Szemere government in 1849. After the war of independence, worked as a historian first in exile and later, after 1867, in Hungary.

Hunyadi, Mátyás (Matthias Corvinus) (1443–1490). Became king of Hungary in 1458, youngest son of János Hunyadi; highly successful ruler both in military exploits and in domestic and economic policy. Also a major supporter of the arts and scholarship.

Illyés, Gyula (1902–1983). Poet and writer, an outstanding figure of twentieth century Hungarian literature. Started contributing to the literary journal *Nyugat* in the 1920s, and became its associate editor in 1937. Attempted to form folk-based culture and promote its values. Edited the journal *Magyar Csillag* from 1941 to 1944. From 1945 was a major figure in the National Peasant Party. Associate editor of the revived journal *Válasz*, 1946–49.

Istóczy, Győző (1842–1915). Lawyer and politician. Member of par liament for the Liberal Party before founding the National Anti-Semitic Party in 1883. Was particularly active during the period of the notorious Tiszaeszlár blood libel case (1883), inciting religious hatred. His articles in his monthly journal *12 Röpirat* [12 Pamphlets] and satirical magazine *Füstölő* [Censer] led to his prosecution for racial incitement.

Jászi, Oszkár (1875–1957). Writer, politician, professor, sociologist. Leading figure and theoretician of Hungarian civic radicalism (universal suffrage, ethnic issue, democratic demands). Minister without portfolio responsible for nationality affairs in the Károlyi government of 1918–19, went into exile during the Hungarian Soviet Republic in 1919 and settled in the USA as a professor of sociology.

Jókai, Mór (1825–1904). Most popular and acclaimed novelist of his time, with a broad following; his works are refined romantic novels, combining romantic passions with anecdotal humor, typically on national themes (portraying the events of the Age of Reform, 1848, and the neoabsolutist era).

Kasztner, Rezső (1906–1957). Born in Kolozsvár [Cluj], a lawyer, journalist and Zionist leader, moved to Budapest in 1940. After many rounds of negotiations, he reached an agreement with the Gestapo to permit 1,684 Jews to escape to Switzerland for a substantial sum. Moved to the Palestine in 1946. In 1954 he sued a journalist who had called him a traitor and a murderer of Jews. Found guilty in the lower court, but in the judgement of the Supreme Court he was guilty of only one charge, of assisting Nazis to escape justice. One year before the case was closed, he was shot dead outside his Tel-Aviv home.

Kazinczy, Ferenc (1759–1831). Writer, linguistic reformer, and literary editor. He set out to modernize and reform the Hungarian language and make it suitable for fine literature. This involved the promotion of strong aesthetic viewpoints, and he corresponded with most of the major Hungarian literary figures of the period.

Kemény, Baron Zsigmond (1814–1875). Writer and politician, peace party member of parliament in 1848–49. An opponent of Hungarian independence, he wrote theoretical antirevolutionary pamphlets in 1850 and 1851, but also disapproved of absolutism. Editor of the newspaper *Pesti Napló* from 1855, and was a supporter of the 1867 Compromise. Better known for the novels he wrote in the 1850s than for his political activity.

Komlós, Aladár (1892–1980). Literary historian, writer, and poet. One of the best-informed, most distinctive critic and essayist on the second generation contributors to the literary journal *Nyugat*. Deported to Bergen-Belsen in 1944. From 1956 to his retirement, independent senior fellow at the Literary History Institute of the Hungarian Academy of Science.

Komlós, János (1922–1980). Officer of the State Defense Authority, (ÁVH) journalist, writer. In charge of the culture section of the dailies *Magyar Nemzet,* and *Népszabadság,* 1958–67. Artistic director of Mikroszkóp Theater from 1967. His criticism and other

articles and satirical engravings appeared in the columns of newspapers and journals.

Kossuth, Lajos (1802–1894). Politician and journalist. Leader of the reform opposition and editor of *Pesti Hírlap* in the 1840s. Minister of finance in the first responsible Hungarian government in 1848, then chairman of the Committee of Defense after the government resigned, then governor of Hungary in 1849, and instrumental in dethroning the House of Habsburg. After the defeat of the revolution, he lived in exile until his death.

Kölcsey, Ferenc (1790–1838). poet, critic, politician. Author of preromantic and patriotic poetry, and the Hungarian national anthem. From 1832 to 1835 Reform Party opposition member of parliament.

Kun, Béla (1886–1939). Communist politician, people's commissar for foreign affairs of the Hungarian Soviet Republic of 1919, fled abroad after its overthrow. Was a member of the Executive Committee of the Comintern in Moscow, 1921–1936.

Lajta, Béla (1873–1920). Architect, internationally-respected representative of modern Hungarian architecture. Folk-national ornamentation is a prominent feature of his early works, but also appears on his later, modern style buildings, such as the Institute for the Blind, the Alms House, the Népszínház Street tenement, and the Malonyi villa.

Lánczy, Leo (1852–1921). Businessman, managing director of Pest Hungarian Commerce Bank in 1881, president of Budapest Chamber of Trade and Industry in 1893. Founder and board member of many large companies. Member of parliament, 1893–1901. Member of the Upper House from 1905. During World War I, organized the war economy together with Ferenc Heinrich.

Lőw, Immánuel (1854–1944). Chief rabbi, orientalist, writer on art history, son of Lipót Lőw. Chief rabbi of the Szeged Jewish congregation 1878. Opposed the White Terror in 1919, for which he was prosecuted in 1921. Gained international recognition for his work on Semitic philology, preaching and botanical work. Translated the Old Testament's Song of Songs into Hungarian. Became member of Upper House in 1927. Deported in 1944, at the age of 90.

Madách, Imre (1823–1864). Poet and writer. Along with József Katona the greatest nineteenth century Hungarian dramatist. His masterpiece, *The Tragedy of Man* (1859–60) towers above his other works.

Marczali, Henrik (1856–1940). Historian and professor. His broad, positivist historiographical output (monographs, many essays, articles, etc.) dealt with both the medieval and modern periods of Hungarian and general history.

Maria Theresia (1717–1780). Crowned queen of Hungary and Bohemia in 1740, and Holy Roman empress in 1745. Notable mainly for her enlightened measures of the 1770s.

Marr, Wilhelm (1818–1904). German anti-Semitic journalist. The first to use the words "Semitic" and "Semitism" instead of "Jewish." Founded the Anti-Semitic League in 1879.

Mocsáry, Lajos (1826–1916). Politician, instrumental in founding the Independence Party. He was its long-time chairman. Notable particularly for his fair ethnic policy views.

Németh, László (1901–1975). Writer and essayist. Most influential ideologist of the populist writers' movement. Propagated a "third road" in place of capitalism and socialism, where the leading role would be played by the Hungarian peasantry and the middle-class arising from it.

Nordau, Max Simon (1849–1923). Journalist and writer, leading figure of modern Zionism. The intellectual leader of the movement from the death of Theodor Herzl in 1904 up to the World War I.

Petőfi, Sándor (1823–1849). Romantic poet. In the 1840s, represented radical innovation on contemporary poetry in terms of subject matter, style and language (simple, folk-song like language, peasant themes). In 1846, started to embrace revolutionary ideals, and his revolutionary poems were also major innovations in contemporary lyric poetry. One of the leaders of the Pest revolution of 1848, fought in the 1848–49 War of Independence. Killed in the Battle of Fehéregyház in 1849. The demotic element of his poetry inspired many imitators from the 1850s onwards.

Podmaniczky, Baron Frigyes (1824–1907). Politician and writer. As chairman of the Budapest Council of Public Works, greatly ad-

vanced the development of the city. Member of parliament 1861–1906. Chairman of the Liberal Party from 1889 to its abolition.

Miklós Radnóti (1909–1944). Poet and translator. In his youth he was influenced by Christian-socialist ideology. The spread of fascism and his presentiment of violent death, evoked from him a steadily strengthening and clarifying voice of combative humanism. Called up to labor service on 20 May 1944. Taken to Serbia, he was marched west during the September retreat, and executed on the road, near Abda. His remains along with his last poems were found in the mass grave in Abda.

Ravasz, László (1882–1975). Calvinist bishop, appointed to Dunamellék diocese in 1921. Member of Upper House, 1927–44. Resigned as bishop in May 1948. During the interwar period, he was a leading figure among that faction of the Hungarian Reformed Church which cooperated with the Horthy regime. Published many essays, literary articles, and sermons.

Reid, Thomas (1710–1796). Scottish philosopher. Founder of the "common sense" school.

Rohling, August (1839–1931). Anti-Semitic theologist. In his infamous book *Der Talmudjude* (1871), he published fake quotations from the Talmud, such as the claim that the Jews use the blood of Christians for their rituals. His doctrines were also built into Nazi ideology.

Solomon (ruled approx. 970–933 BC). Son of David, third king of Israel. His wisdom is often presented through the "judgements of Solomon." Ancient Israel flourished under his reign. His greatest work was the Temple in Jerusalem, which stood until 586. Tradition ascribes to him the books of the Old Testament Proverbs, Song of Songs, and Ecclesiastes.

Schwab, Löw (1794–1857). Chief rabbi of Pest. Conservative in theology, he permitted as much reform as was absolutely necessary in ritual. He founded the Jewish Hospital and the Dohány Street Synagogue. Spent twelve weeks in the Újépület prison for his activities during the 1848–49 War of Independence.

Sík, Sándor (1889–1963). Poet, translator, literary historian, and writer of religious literature, professor. Provincial head of the Piarist order in 1948. Edited the journal *Vigilia* from 1946. His verses,

which broke through the bounds of ecclesiastical poetry, also dealt with the problems of modern society. His works on literary history and aesthetics feature a highly refined analysis.

Smith, Adam (1723–1790). Scottish philosopher, social scientist, and economist. The basis of his economic theory is the principle of laissez faire: the public good is best promoted by the behavior of economic players in following their own interests, so that state intervention must be restricted to a very narrow area.

Stern, Samu (1874–1946). President of the Pest Jewish congregation 1929. Under his leadership, the Pest Jewish congregation merged with the central Hungarian Neolog organization, the National Jewish Office. On 25 March 1944, he was appointed president of the Jewish Council.

Szabolcsi, Lajos (1889–1943). Deputy editor of *Egyenlőség* [Equality] 1911, and editor 1915. In the early 1920s, together with Vilmos Vázsonyi and Chief Rabbi Simon Hevesi, founded the Central Jewish Student Aid Committee. After the closure of *Egyenlőség* in 1938, worked for the *Magyar Zsidók Lapja* [Journal of Hungarian Jews].

Szálasi, Ferenc (1897–1946). Army officer, organizer of the Hungarian Arrow Cross movement in the 1930s. Became "leader of the nation" through a coup in October 1944, and arranged total military and economic mobilization to support the German occupation. Sentenced to death as a war criminal in 1946 by the People's Court.

Széchenyi, Count István (1791–1860). Politician, writer on economics. From the 1820s to 1848, the prime mover in the adoption of civilizing and infrastructural institutions and middle-class innovations. Minister of transport in the first responsible Hungarian government in April–September 1848. His views diverged from the aims of the Hungarian revolution at many points. Entered a mental asylum in September 1848 and stayed there, withdrawn from active life, until his suicide.

Szemere, Bertalan (1812–1869). Politician, prime minister, writer. Interior minister in the first responsible Hungarian government, then member of the National Defense Committee, and after the dethronement (May–September 1849), prime minister and inte-

rior minister. After the 1848–49 Revolution and War of Independence, lived in exile almost until his death.

Szép, Ernő (1884–1953). Poet and writer. First made his mark as a contributor of poetry to *Nyugat*. His naïve forms of expression and refined poetic language was coupled with a distinctive Budapest character. His cabaret sketches and plays were also widely popular.

Teleki, Count Pál (1879–1941). Politician, prime minister, geography professor and notorious anti-Semite. Director of the Geographical Institute 1909–13. During the Horthy era, several times appointed minister of culture, foreign affairs, and twice prime minister (19 July 1920–13 April 1921, and 16 February 1939–3 April 1941). Urged that Hungarian revisionist demands be pressed. When World War II broke out, represented the policy of "armed neutrality," and on perceiving this to be untenable, committed suicide on 3 April 1941.

Vas, István (1910–1991). Poet, writer, translator, member of the third generation of *Nyugat*. Drafted into labor service in the early 1940s. At the end of the World War II, hid with the help of his wife and friends. Prohibited from publishing between 1949 and 1953, and was criticized at the Hungarian Writer's Union meetings.

Vázsonyi, Vilmos (1868–1926). Lawyer, minister, politician. Minister of justice, 1917–18. After the collapse of the Hungarian Soviet Republic in 1919, worked first as a royalist politician, then 1924 became an organizer of the Democratic Bloc, which included part of the left-wing opposition.

Vida, Jenő (1872–1945). Industrialist, managing director of the Hungarian Coal Mines Company. He had strong links to the Hungarian General Credit Bank, the Aluminium Ore Mine and Industry Company and many other industrial firms. As an industrialist, he supported the political establishment, and became member of the Upper House in 1927. He was deported to Auschwitz following the German occupation of Hungary in 1944.

Vörösmarty, Mihály (1800–1855). Poet and dramatist. His works brought him fame and acclaim from the 1820s onwards. His work embraced great verse epics, verse dramas, and lyric poetry. Best known as the author of *Szózat* (considered the second

national anthem) and of romantic verses on the fate of the nation and mankind.

WEININGER, OTTO (1880–1903). Austrian philosopher and psychologist. After gaining his doctorate, converted from Judaism to Christianity. His book *Geschlecht und Charakter* (1903) was used in anti-Semitic propaganda. The basis of his thinking was that the masculine element was positive, productive, and moral, as against the negative, unproductive and immoral female element. The Jews, interpreted as being the carriers of feminine aspects, thus represented immorality in contrast to Christianity. Committed suicide in Vienna.

WEISS, BARON MANFRÉD (1857–1922). Leading figure of Hungarian manufacturing industry. Founded the first Hungarian ammunition factory in Csepel in 1892. After World War I, shifted to the production of agricultural machinery, enamel pots, bicycles, sewing machines and other items, and then founded textile, aircraft, and motorcycle factories. Member of Upper House 1915, ennobled in 1918.

ZELK, ZOLTÁN (1906–1981). Poet and writer. Arrested several times for his political views during the Horthy era. Sent to Ukraine on labor service 1942–44. Put his pen at the service of the Communist system during the 1948–53. In 1956 he belonged to the revolutionary group in the Hungarian Writer's Union. Convicted in 1957, but amnestied in October 1958.

ZUKOR, ADOLF (1873–1976). Hungarian-born film magnate, emigrated to America at the age of sixteen. He set up a cinema chain, then founded the film company Famous Players in 1912. Following a series of mergers, became president of Paramount Pictures in 1916 and held that post until 1936.

ZWEIG, STEFAN (1881–1942). Austrian writer and poet. Following the rise of Nazism in Austria, fled to London, and settled in Brazil in 1940. The dismal prospects of the World War II and his own exiled existence led him to commit suicide. One of the most widely-read interwar German-language authors.

PHOTOGRAPHS

Mór Ballagi

Vilmos Fraknói

Max Simon Nordau

Vilmos Vázsonyi

Oszkár Jászi

Béla Kun

Immánuel Lőw

Miklós Radnóti

INDEX

ABOUT THE AUTHOR

ANDRÁS GERŐ is professor of history, and chairman of the Department of History at Budapest University (ELTE). He is also professor of history at Central European University, and the director of the Institute of Habsburg History. He has published widely in Hungarian, as well as in English and German. His recent English-language publications include *The Hungarian Parliament (1867–1918): A Mirage of Power* (1997), *Emperor Francis Joseph, King of the Hungarians* (2001), and *Imagined History. Chapters from Nineteenth and Twentieth Century Hungarian Symbolic Politics* (2006).

BOOKS PUBLISHED BY THE CENTER FOR HUNGARIAN STUDIES AND PUBLICATIONS

CHSP Hungarian Authors Series:

No. 1. *False Tsars*. Gyula Szvák. 2000.

No. 2. *Book of the Sun*. Marcell Jankovics. 2001.

No. 3. *The Dismantling of Historic Hungary: The Peace Treaty of Trianon, 1920*. Ignác Romsics. 2002.

No. 4. *The Soviet and Hungarian Holocausts: A Comparative Essay.* Tamás Krausz. 2006.

CHSP Hungarian Studies Series:

No. 1. *Emperor Francis Joseph, King of the Hungarians*. András Gerő. 2001.

No. 2. *Global Monetary Regime and National Central Banking. The Case of Hungary, 1921–1929*. György Péteri. 2002.

No. 3. *Hungarian-Italian Relations in the Shadow of Hitler's Germany, 1933–1940*. György Réti. 2003.

No. 4. *The War Crimes Trial of Hungarian Prime Minister László Bárdossy*. Pál Pritz. 2004.

No. 5. *Identity and the Urban Experience: Fin-de-Siècle Budapest.* Gábor Gyáni. 2004.

No. 6. *Picturing Austria-Hungary. The British Perception of the Habsburg Monarchy, 1865–1870.* Tibor Frank. 2005.

No. 7. *Anarchism in Hungary: Theory, History, Legacies.* András Bozóki and Miklós Sükösd. 2006.

No. 8. *Myth and Remembrance. The Dissolution of the Habsburg Empire in the Memoir Literature of the Austro-Hungarian Political Elite.* Gergely Romsics. 2006.

No. 9. *Imagined History. Chapters from Nineteenth and Twentieth Century Hungarian Symbolic Politics.* András Gerő. 2006.

No. 10. *Pál Teleki (1874–1941). The Life of a Controversial Hungarian Politician.* Balázs Ablonczy. 2006.

No. 11. *The Hungarian Revolution of 1956. Myths and Realities.* László Eörsi. 2006.

No. 12. *The Jewish Criterion in Hungary.* András Gerő. 2007.